# Being With Cows

# Being With Cows

DAVE MOUNTJOY

Bedford Square
Publishers

First published in the UK in 2024 by Bedford Square Publishers Ltd,
London, UK

bedfordsquarepublishers.co.uk
@bedsqpublishers

A CIP catalogue record for this book is available from the British Library.

Typeset by Palimpsest Book Production Limited, Falkirk, Stirlingshire

Printed in Great Britain by CPI Group (UK) Ltd, Croydon CRO 4YY

ISBN
978-1-83501-034-1 (Hardback)
978-1-83501-035-8 (eBook)

2 4 6 8 10 9 7 5 3 1

*For Judith, you shining Saint of a spotless Casta.*

# Contents

# Prologue

I love animals. It's as simple as that really. Above all else I love them for the way in which they remind me of quietness; they seem to have an existence largely untroubled by thought. They are as they are, without need for reflection or introspection.

As far as I'm aware and with increasing conviction, I can say that theirs is a life lived mindfully. They are natural experts, born to be and not to think about being. Perhaps they are the lucky ones?

Perhaps I have been lucky myself, privileged to be able to spend so much precious time in their company, the cats and dogs and cows and calves, puppies and childhood guinea pigs?

I must have been in my mid to late twenties, still living very happily at home with mum and dad, when a family friend brought three jackdaw chicks to the house. I can't say why but somehow their arrival made me think of our own family brood, especially my two brothers Pete and Cork – one chick for each of us. The bringer of such unexpected innocence into our midst was a local woodcutter and genuine salt-of-the-earth material. He had found the three little waifs still in the nest, a relatively rough old affair of twigs and bits and pieces that the parents had found round about. He'd been asked to clear the chimneys of a rambling old country house of such unwanted things, but hadn't had the heart to knock the little ones on the head.

Knowing that our family was well known in the area for taking in injured wild birds or animals, he had decided to bring them, very much alive and kicking, to us. We happily took them in and, looking at their soft black downy feathers, we guessed that they were a couple of weeks old at the most. Jackdaw chicks fledge at around four to five weeks and therefore with at least two or three weeks until they could be returned to the wild, we popped them in the quietest shed in the garden, out of harm's way from magpies, jays and the host of neighbouring cats. Their new nest was an old fruit box full of straw and they seemed to take to it immediately without any fuss at all.

The next days in their company can only be described as an absolute delight. Gorging themselves on bread and milk as often as they liked, the chicks grew strong and incredibly confident. What amazed us all was the intimacy that they were capable of expressing. Once their tummies were full, they would hop on to the nearest hand, bounce their way up the arm and settle so comfortably in the crook of the chosen one's neck. When it was my turn to receive such a blessing, I would go into raptures as a small but inquisitive little beak would ever so softly begin exploring the inside of one of my ears. What an absolute privilege to share such moments with such beautifully alive little beings.

When the shed door was finally left open for good, the fledgelings spent the first few days in and around the garden. They would still come to be fed and were happy to perch on the head, hand, arm or shoulder but little by little they began to edge further afield. The day came, not long after, when they seemed to have flown the nest for good. For several days I would go out into the field, calling out to them in the hope that they would return for a final goodbye. It must've been a month later, as August gave way to September, that I thought I would try just one more time. Walking right up to the far edge of the field, I thought I could hear several jackdaws chattering away in some old oaks a couple of hundred yards away from where I was standing. 'Jack, Jack, Jack, come on then Jack, come on then.' After five minutes without response, I turned to go back to the house. I hadn't really expected anything to happen but thought it was worth a try. As I reached the middle of the meadow, something made me turn and look back towards the trees. To my utter amazement and joy, I saw three young jackdaws heading directly towards me. Stretching my arms out as I had done in the garden several weeks before, I waited to see what would happen. Barely able to breathe with the excitement that had gripped me, I continued to hold out my arms until one after another, those beautiful black forms just swept right in and landed with perfect poise and precision on my outstretched limbs.

Even after so many years, I have yet to find the words

to adequately describe the sense of belonging and trust that I experienced during those moments. The intelligence behind their strikingly light blue eyes, the outlandish way in which they hopped from my head to shoulders and back again had me feeling that I was in the presence of an expression of pure love. I was lit up inside, totally dissolved in the sheer naturalness of their antics. Every single comic twist of their blue-black heads, the jester-like way in which they peered into my disbelieving face, brought a confirmation of nature's capacity to stir up very deep feelings of both gratitude and humility.

After this final goodbye, I never saw the jackdaws up close again. It didn't matter. What they had gifted me was precious beyond words. That they were successfully returned to the wild was the icing on the cake. To have tried to have kept them as pets would have spoken of attachment and it simply couldn't be that way.

Experiences such as this one have ingrained in me a reverence for the natural world. Once a refuge, I now see it as the purest expression of Life itself. There is something inherently whole and revealing to be found among the trees and meadows and streams. Revealing in the sense that with patience and commitment, the dedicated searcher can come to realise the futility of thought and foolishness of a reliance upon its flimsy fiction of a world.

By its very nature, the natural world provides a constant reminder that nothing in this appearing world can lay claim to any sort of permanence. A fallen tree that rots slowly back into the forest floor, the thousandth pheasant that day to be levelled into the unyielding tarmac of a busy road or even the side of an immovable mountain that slid to the valley floor are all testament to the constant change and ebb and flow of Life's great singular movement.

However, behind the façade of apparent form, there lies the very essence of what we mistakenly call *our* lives – namely the source of absolute quietness, the unmoving and unmovable Is-ness of being that exists as the very heart of mindfulness.

When I look quietly into the liquid eyes of any of the cows we share the farm with, I am immediately reminded of an inescapable sense of stillness. There is something so uncomplicated in the bright-shine which calls me back through memory and thought itself, until the very idea of a separate *me* becomes nothing more than a figment of a limited and ultimately finite imagination.

The red and roe deer, the wild boar, pine marten and *chat forestier* are but a few of our nearest neighbours in this little upland chunk of paradise. It is to them we look for inspiration. It is they who remind us of our place in the world and that quietness really is king. While it's a treat indeed to see them going about their business, their presence is most appreciated from an interior perspective.

The blue tit, wren and tiny goldcrest struggling to survive in the hungry months of winter speak to me of courage. The thrushes who start all over again when late frost takes their featherless brood are reminders of determination. Even the stream in the valley bottom, gurgling in spring's rain-filled generosity and dry under cloudless skies of August heat, nudges me into accepting the fleeting nature of what appears to be so solid and reliable a world.

# CHAPTER I

# Direction

'Sometimes in the wind of change we find our true direction.'

ANON

For several years, beginning in 2006, I became a regular visitor to the Findhorn Foundation (a spiritual community founded in the late 1960s) in northern Scotland, hell-bent on making the absolute most of having no other commitment in life but that of self-discovery. Yes, it IS a commitment.

It was on what was to be the final journey north in 2012 that this solo voyage came to its natural conclusion, for during those late-summer days along the Moray Firth, I met the woman who was to become my wife.

'Hello. I'm Diana. I come from Barcelona,' and then several days later, 'Where have you been? I was looking for you.'

When the workshop ended, we agreed to meet up in Spain, first of all in Avila and then continuing across the French Pyrenees, from the Atlantic to the Mediterranean coasts. Soon after meeting, we had discovered a mutual desire to live in the Pyrenees and it was with this in mind that we travelled. For several weeks, we meandered back and forth across the border between France and Spain. Both of us felt most at home and inspired by the area on the French side known as the Couserans, in the department of the Ariège. Perhaps the wildest part of the French Pyrenees and still populated by a small number of European brown bears, the steeply carved valleys, majestic beech woodlands and snow-capped mountain peaks cast a deeply intoxicating spell on us.

There is something so very humbling *and* invigorating to be found in the presence of such mountainous majesty. For a while, we explored without thought of making home, content to simply be there, grateful that we had time to wander at leisure.

At the beginning of 2013, as the first real snow of winter made a wonderland of both mountain and valley, we rented a small place right in the heart of the Couserans. By now we were sure that it was here or round abouts that we wanted to live. There was a sense of fertility, of lush greenery and the freshest of air that was somehow lacking once we stepped outside the mountains themselves. Even the Piedmont, the foothills and rolling hills around, still breathtakingly beautiful and deeply wooded, failed to ignite in us the fire we that felt beside those rocky peaks.

Using the rented flat as a base, we searched and we searched, from cottage to ruin and everything in-between, yet as Life would have it, the place that for both of us ticked all our many boxes, failed to materialise. Too much traffic, too expensive or not enough land, there was always something that prevented both of us from saying a definite yes.

Frustration. Arguments: tantrums and threats to abandon the whole adventure.

We did give up for a while, spending the spring of 2013 in Morocco, laying the foundations of a relationship that was to be sorely tested in the months and years to come.

Yet we never gave up completely. Something kept us hanging in there, trusting, *trusting* that all would eventually be well.

Landing back in south-western France the following autumn, we started to look further afield and after much deliberation, decided to rent some land and eco-cabins near the market town of Saint-Girons. At the end of a twisting three-mile track, if it was isolation we wanted, we had it in plenty. Two lovingly crafted natural buildings, woodland and meadow and a view that seemed to stretch to the ends of the world. The sunsets were simply spellbinding. No mains water, no inside toilet and most definitely no Internet, via landline, signal or any other means. It was what you might call interesting!

Our plan at the time was to develop a glamping business on the land. We were convinced that the beauty of the landscape and in particular the staggering views west to where the sun dipped down would be enough to have guests pouring in. Two yurts were ordered from an English couple who had settled nearby in the mountains. Diana began to make beautiful flyers and a website for what we hoped would become a thriving enterprise.

But Life! Things just happen as they do, regardless of ideas or carefully crafted plans. Diana became pregnant and the more I worked on the land, preparing things for the eventual opening of the glampsite, the more I was bothered by the fact that we didn't actually own it. I felt restricted, somehow, subject to the whims of the owner's plans and preferences. As the autumn gave way to winter and snow blocked the track for weeks at a time, that sense of not being Lord and Lady of our own manor really began to nag away at me. I couldn't find the confidence I was looking for to reassure me that all the investments we were making in the place, beautiful as it was, would eventually bear fruit.

At the beginning of 2014, I began looking again for a property that would allow us to refine and then develop our ideas into a concrete plan and vision. Mirepoix, a small town in the very north-east of the department, was not somewhere we had passed through before. Well out of the mountains and with more of a Mediterranean climate than the freshness of Saint-Girons and the Pyrenees further west, we had not considered that such a place could be somewhere we could settle and thrive.

So much for plans and deeply held desires. One look at the view from the top of some organic land we went to see nearby was enough. 'This is it!' I said to Diana. I didn't need to think about it. It would have been such a shame to *think* when faced with such a view – a wave of forested greenery whose foaming crest seemed to come crashing down at the feet of the mountains themselves. It was just so complete and staggeringly beautiful that to think would have been akin to some kind of blasphemy and I knew without a shadow of doubt that the search had come to its end. Diana, however, wasn't completely convinced, and even the spontaneous jig of delight with which I celebrated did little to soothe her worries. Although the 75 acres were indeed picture-postcard perfect and two beautiful wooden barns were included in the sale, the fact of the matter was that there was no house to live in. Where would we stay, she asked? Would we have to rent nearby? How much would that cost? At the time, we couldn't afford the extra burden of having to rent somewhere on top of the actual purchase of the land.

I listened to her concerns, her genuine worries, the proper questions to be asked by a heavily pregnant mother-to-be, but I just couldn't pull my eyes from the view. Something was insisting. It wasn't stubbornness or even that I'd fallen so quickly in love with the land, but something not easily definable that had me rooted to the spot. 'This is it,' I repeated. 'We have to take the plunge and here is where we dive in.' We talked for a while about risk and the more we gave voice to our feelings, any lingering doubts that I may have unknowingly had about the place evaporated. It wasn't a case of trying to persuade Diana or convince her that everything would be OK. I couldn't even offer such meagre words of comfort. As I saw it at the time, the greatest risk lay in denial, in a refusal to listen to what something beyond the chit-chat patter of thought was telling me. As long as I kept this in mind, there was nothing else to say. The quietness I was experiencing said it all and words would only serve to get in the way. Within an hour or two, on the way back to Saint-Girons, it seemed like Diana had intuited this rock-like refusal to budge as a sign that risks were for the taking. She spoke very little but gave her consent to the plan.

The first days we spent on the land are difficult to describe. It was mid-April, only two short months from that first heady visit, yet now that spring was in full spate, the whole landscape had changed. Winter's stark scrawl had swelled to bursting point, a humid riot of unfolding green that spoke of warmth and the promise of new things to come. Several species of orchid blessed the meadows with their presence, thousands of them turning whole acres into places of holy communion. There were wildflowers everywhere, in the woods, the meadows and skirting the sides of the stream. From the top of the land, the Pyrenees stretched out in an unbroken chain, sometimes smooth and whale-backed, others jagged broken-toothed affairs, yet all still snow-capped at the peaks.

Visually speaking, I was amazed at the transformation that had taken place since the last time we'd visited: amazed and deeply delighted. But what really got me was the sheer mass of sounds that now filled the valley so full of vitality that the air itself seemed to crackle and hum. From crickets to cuckoos and hardy cicadas to the first flocks of swifts screeching happily overhead, the air fizzed with a tangible sense of awakening, of creation cranking sweetly back into action after months of heavy slumber. The jewel in the crown for me was the chorus of croaking frogs who nightly lulled me into some of the deepest and cleanest of sleeps I could remember. Only in Africa had I heard such intense expression, the season singing itself into being.

As orchestras go, this surely topped the lot and several times during those first few days, my gratitude at being brought to such a place brought tears to the eyes. I felt so much at home that it seemed like the landscape was merely an extension of my own body.

Where had the risk been? If fortune favours the brave, then already we had been repaid for our trust in the process in ways that made money seem such a poor indicator of wealth. These were real riches, breathable vibrating outpourings of nature's greenest gold.

Such was the depth of the feeling I had that all was unfolding as Life intended that it was no surprise when the previous owners offered us a wooden chalet to live in free of charge, on the edge of the land we'd bought from them. From all around came confirmation that as mere pawns on the chessboard of Life, we were being moved into very favourable positions.

As the first week in our role of new guardians of the land came to a close, Diana and myself began to settle into some kind of routine. In between mealtimes, we would explore the farm, immersing ourselves in all it had to offer. I was thrilled to find that we shared the land with such a rich array of wildlife: foxes, badgers, wild boar, red and roe deer and even the elusive genet. We also kept an eye out for potential yurt sites because at that time glamping was still the heartbeat of the project.

Several weeks passed by in an excited blur of discovery. Spring gave way to summer and with it came the sense of something reaching its peak. The meadows were awash with colour and the migrant birds a constant source of wonder: bee-eaters, hoopoes and door-sized vultures circling high overhead had me in raptures. It was everything I could have ever wished for, a veritable Aladdin's Cave of natural treasure, and it was into this mix that *they* first found their way into the conversation.

I was sitting one evening with Francis, the previous owner of the land and now our nearest neighbour. My French was at the very best what you might call minimal, but I felt so warm and relaxed in his company that the words didn't seem to really matter at all. When I'd told him a few weeks before that I'd seen a sheep standing high up on the roof of the barn, an impressive forty feet from the ground, he'd taken it all in his stride, acting as if it was the most normal thing in the world. I can't remember what I'd actually wanted to tell him but whatever was lost in translation only helped to cement the bond between us.

On this occasion, he had asked me about our plans for the land and, in particular, where we wanted to live in the long-term. The chalet, as convenient as it was, was at best a glorified shed. I tried to tell him that, as yet, we hadn't given the matter serious thought, so intent were we in getting the glamping business up and running. Without beating around the proverbial bush, he suggested that one of the wooden barns that he himself had built was ripe for conversion into a beautiful home. He also told me, with an unmistakable glint in his eye, that the best way to go about getting permission was to become an *agriculteur*, a farmer of one sort or another, whose activity required a permanent presence on the land. He and his wife Flo had followed the very same path in order to get planning permission for their incredible off-grid farmhouse.

Having spent most of my childhood on my mum's family cattle farm, I was immediately comfortable with the idea of having some livestock around, even if the rapidly evolving plan had them pencilled in as mere stepping-stones towards the conversion of one of the barns. Animals hadn't featured at all in any of our previous discussions, but now that a seed had been planted, I quickly warmed to the idea. I even found a quote that seemed to sum up quite perfectly this unexpected change in direction: 'Every now and then one paints a picture that seems to have opened a door and serves as a stepping-stone to other things.' At the time, Pablo Picasso's words were interpreted with a home in mind. The picture I envisaged was of a small scattering of animals, enough to receive the planning permission, but nothing more. Little did I know quite how prophetic the great master's words would turn out to be.

Not sheep or goats or pigs and not fruit or vegetables either, but cows. It had to be cows. They were the lifeblood of mum's farm and I'd grown up in their company. Chasing, being chased, feeding, bleeding and at times trembling with fear, my experience of life at a young age was very much coloured by their cloven-hoofed presence. When Diana and I had taken Francis' suggestion to heart and agreed that I would register as an official *exploitant agricole*, it seemed that I'd come full circle, returning, however unexpectedly, to my roots. I was quietly happy that events had taken such an unimagined turn and secretly content that it should be with cows that we moved our project forward.

# CHAPTER 2

# It's all about the cows

'Cows are amongst the gentlest of breathing creatures; none show more passionate tenderness to their young when deprived of them; and, in short, I am not ashamed to profess a deep love for these quiet creatures.'

THOMAS DE QUINCEY

The first three heifers arrived in January 2015. On a bitterly cold day, Diana, myself and Gabi, our gurgling six-month-old son, fetched them from a beautiful farm high up in the foothills of the French Alps, near Gap. I don't

know what it was that had persuaded me to go for Galloways, a hardy ancient breed from the Scottish borders, and to drive so far when the landscape around Mirepoix was sprinkled with an assortment of cattle farms. The fact that I didn't question such an apparently illogical decision was an early indication of just how deeply the cows were going to affect me. It seems that their non-thinking presence was already beginning to exert a powerful influence, and that their own quiet version of logic ran along very different lines to my generally accepted definition of the word.

Once we got them back to the farm, everything began to change, immediately. I had been excited about creating the glamping business. The prospect of balancing the books by sharing such an idyllic tucked-away piece of living Pyrenean tapestry was something I felt good about. We'd already built the wooden platforms on which the yurts were to be sited and had started work on the toilet and shower block. But with the cows came something of a different quality, more subtle by far yet somehow still earthy and wholly organic.

The idea for the glamping site had come through a series of brainstorming sessions, in which Diana and I had jotted down a mass of thoughts, covering sheet after sheet with everything ranging from fears and phobias to ambitions and the way we wanted to live.

Not a single word was ever written about animals, cows included, but now that they were here, well, I might as well have taken the biggest marker pen I could find and crossed out almost everything I'd previously agreed to.

They hadn't been part of any mind map, simply because, as I was soon to discover, they operated outside what I normally considered to be the mind – the world of thoughts and mental activity that dictated the rhythm of virtually every waking moment.

For the first six weeks, Isi, July and Valentine, as the Galloways were called, were kept in one of the barns that we hoped their presence would help us convert into a home. It was love at first sight and I delighted in taking Gabi with me. I would sit on a bale outside their pen with sleeping beauty in my arms. It was a sheer delight to be sandwiched between two such slices of wholemeal goodness. If Diana took Gabi to see her family in Spain, I would sit there for hours, mostly free of thought and content to be breathing the same air. They fascinated me and made me laugh. Above everything else, they made me smile in much the same way that Gabi did. There was an innocence about them, an honesty that I found highly seductive, and I became, I suppose, an addict of some kind, dosing up on a daily fix of bovine benevolence.

The more time I spent with them, the more I came to know their characters. Valentine was clearly the boss. She was first to each pile of fresh hay and the least timid of the three. Isi and July seemed tied equal second. Even though they were so few in number, I was amazed at their acceptance of this social structure and that for them it was simply the natural order of things. Perhaps that was the first real insight they gave me – that acceptance is a key to the unlocking of many quiet doors. I could see that the hierarchy to which they conformed allowed them to exist in relative harmony, even in such a confined space as the barn. During those early days, I didn't see them as teachers, yet simply by being themselves, they imparted a wisdom that I couldn't help but absorb.

It was during another conversation with Francis in my mangled French that I first came to hear of the Casta, a fabled breed of cattle that came originally from the very heart of the French Pyrenees. Surly, stubborn and difficult to do business with, they carried a reputation of non-compliance and barely concealed rebelliousness. He told me that he'd toyed with the idea of keeping a few Casta, a couple of mothers who he could milk by hand or oxen, perhaps, with whom he could work in the forest, pulling out trees he'd felled in inaccessible places. He also wanted to help save them, as the breed had become critically endangered since the modernisation of agriculture took hold at the end of the Second World War.

I was intrigued with what he told me, and that very evening I took what proved to be the first steps into what might be called the Castaverse, a journey from which I've yet to return. Within minutes of typing their name into the search box of *Leboncoin*, a French version of eBay, I discovered that there was a whole herd for sale just 20km away from the farm. Coincidence? No mate, no such thing. I laughed as I read through the advert: a fair price, organically certified and ready to go immediately.

A week later, on another cold and sleety Pyrenean day, we slowly snaked our way along an impossibly twisting lane that meandered this way and that through some forgotten backwater of the foothills. On arriving at the farm, we were taken straight into the gloomy, ill-lit shed that contained what seemed at first glance to be a swirling nervous mass of hoof and horn.

A swarm of frightened bees came to mind, flashing out their barely concealed fear in a series of rapid, reactive movements. The farmer was all smiles and full of good humour, yet the twenty or so young heifers that he had for sale reflected something far less welcoming and warm.

We stood for some time just looking into the pen. For such a cold, murky day and in such poorly lit conditions, the atmosphere inside the shed was surprisingly loaded. The constant skittishness of the Casta acted like some kind of dynamo or generator, filling the air with a very raw and unpredictable energy.

Several times I thought some of the youngsters might take flight and sail clear over the gates that kept them locked inside. It was almost painfully obvious that they weren't used to being so contained and some of the faces showed sure signs of distress.

I had already told the farmer upon arrival that we wanted to take three heifers off him but when, after half an hour inside the shed, he asked me which ones we were interested in, it was a job to separate one from another, so tightly packed together were they in an ever-shifting circle, let alone decide which ones would come and live near Mirepoix.

However, I'd already noticed that there were three, a little group within the group, who were even more edgy and uneasy than the rest. They were smaller, too, and less well-formed. They never managed to burrow their way into the relative safety that lay at the centre of the circle, so I had a good view of them each time the movement of the herd brought them past us.

I can't really say what brought me to tell the farmer that we would take them. He looked surprised at first, surprised and in some way secretly relieved that here was someone prepared to take what looked distinctly like the runts of the whole group.

There was just something about them that pulled me. I certainly didn't feel any pity for what appeared to be the three skinniest waifs imaginable, no honourable sense of compassion or kind-hearted do-gooding. Some happenings are best left unmolested by words and are perhaps most accurately explained by an absence of detail and description. That it was simply meant to be is the best I can do at this moment.

Even during that first contact with them, I couldn't fail to see how alert they were, and I left with the impression that they wore domestication like some ill-fitting robe, which they could jump out of at any moment. If the Galloways expressed a sense of being solidly grounded and firm, these things were all electricity and sensitive beyond belief.

On the way back home to Mirepoix, I experienced a surge of some undefined excitement and was left feeling that I'd been touched by something pure and perfectly clean. And that evening back in the chalet, sitting quietly in front of the fire, I instinctively understood that the Casta demanded transparency. I was reflecting on how some of them we'd seen earlier had had such a deeply penetrating look in their eyes – not necessarily borne of fear but of something wild and elemental, even. As I poked at the embers, I had the clear impression that there would be no hiding place to be found in their midst. Little did I know how accurate these intuitive insights would prove to be.

Judith, Jacinthe and Jalie arrived towards the end of February. The Galloways had been turned out onto the land and the Casta took their place in the barn. Where a week before there had been three plump and docile choirgirls, we now had a trio of brooding teenagers, gaunt, incredibly nervous and already, probably, looking for the exit. Chalk and cheese came to mind. The atmosphere in and around the barn had gone from a veritable love-in to something supercharged with caution and a deep sense of reservation. They would have absolutely nothing to do with me, backing away into the farthest corner of the pen whenever I approached. Unlike the Galloways, who had let me get in there among them right from the very start, the Casta were constantly on the back foot, refusing my every attempt to build bridges between us.

After a week of being persistently shunned, it began to dawn on me that perhaps I was a little out of my depth. None of the normal approaches had worked – neither the softly voiced repetition of simple words, nor the attempts to court favour by offering such treats as salt or handfuls of oats. On my mum's farm, I'd never encountered such resistance and I have to say it unsettled me. I desperately wanted to reach out to them and touch them, scaling the walls of extreme aloofness that I felt were keeping us from each other.

That they wouldn't let me in began to become a source of irritation. Keeping me at arm's length had certainly been a blow to my ego. I'd considered myself to be something of a Saint Francis as far as animals were concerned, someone to be instinctively trusted. Having this bubble burst was deflating.

The standoff continued into the second week. I was trying my best to be patient, to trust that little by little I would win their confidence and we could at the very least establish a mutual respect that would make working with them less unpredictable or even dangerous.

I say dangerous with good reason. One afternoon during that period, Diana and I had been working at the other end of the barn, clearing out some old stuff that the previous owners had left behind. At some point we started to argue. A heated discussion became a full-blown slanging match and for a brief moment, our raised voices echoed round the valley. Diana returned to the chalet. I ambled over to check on the Casta and noticed that the water in the trough was getting low. Within seconds of entering the pen with a fresh bucket, one of them went for me. Head down, horns up, she flew across the gap between us. I just about managed to hurdle the gate before she came crashing into it.

I was stunned. It wasn't supposed to be like this. What the hell was going on? It was only when I began to calm down that the first faint inkling of understanding trickled gently into awareness. My appreciation of just how impossibly sensitive the Casta were was suddenly raised to unknown heights. All my own reservations about them simply fell away in that moment of clarity and I looked at them cowering almost in one corner through new, deeply grateful eyes. More than anything else I felt humbled, privileged to be in their presence.

Being charged had been nothing short of a blessing in disguise, for in the intensity of the moment and the rattling of my chains that followed, I had seen that the Casta, in their purity, were mirrors of a most spotless kind, bouncing back everything I brought to them. When I entered the pen after the argument with Diana, the attack was simply their way of returning what I'd screeched out into the air around us. It was as if they were saying, 'Here you go; this is what it looks like, you know, the anger and all that'. Everything suddenly fell into place and all the frustration and annoyance made perfect sense. Of course, they were going to be timid, reserved and standoffish when, deep down, I was the one who was bringing such stuff to their doorstep. The Bible, via a teenage Bob Marley, sang out loud and clear in my head: *Judge not, before you judge yourself.*

In the following days, going to see the Casta became something like making a trip to the temple. It's not that I fell down on my knees in an act of worship, but inside myself there was most definitely a deep appreciation of their sanctity and ability to shine a light right down into my darkest nooks and crannies. To be with them, to really be with them, required that an effort be made, a commitment to keeping quiet, undisturbed by the mass of thoughts and feelings that wriggled around inside me.

On the surface, the Casta seemed as aloof as ever and when, a few weeks later, they too were turned out onto the meadows, they immediately disappeared into the woodland, seeking refuge among the oaks and ashes and wild cherry. What *had* changed so dramatically was awareness of what I was carrying inside me, whether I was with them or not. After years of yoga, meditation and a kind of haphazard freestyle form of introspection, I'd finally encountered something of what I felt to be unshakeable solidity, a living honesty in the form of the three long-legged beauties. These things were the real deal.

It's pretty safe to say that this was the beginning of the end of the whole glamping adventure. After the cows arrived, it moved further and further into the background, eventually dying an unnoticed death among the cow muck and bales of hay. The whole project had suddenly taken a most unexpected turn. They'd walked right in, swishing their tails behind them, and stolen the show. What could I do? I loved the yurts and their capacity to cocoon us in a sense of well-rounded cosiness and peace, but the cows, well, this was the beginning of a completely different story. In the space of less than a couple of months, they'd trampled all over our canvas-white plans to such an extent that I could barely think about anything else but them. I suppose I began to suffer, most happily, from a severe form of cow-mania. The magnetic pull they exerted on me was equal to that which I was experiencing with Gabi. In many ways, it seemed like the two were singing from the same hymn sheet and I simply couldn't get enough of the innocent transparency they offered.

It's all about the cows

Diana and I did have one more discussion about the glamping, but it was a no-go from the start. My heart just wasn't in it and although I knew its demise would usher in a period of financial difficulty, I couldn't and wouldn't be diverted from the path that I suddenly found myself following, for as I said to Diana at the end of the conversation, 'It's all about the cows.'

# CHAPTER 3

# Natural practice

'Look deep into nature, and then you will understand everything better.'

ALBERT EINSTEIN

The eureka moment I'd experienced with the cows, the realisation that they were to be at the very heart of whatever project may unfold on the farm, was in some ways akin to the sudden damming of a stream at the very peak of its flow. Having finally found a place that satisfied us both, Diana and myself had been carried along on a wave of excitement, drunk almost on the possibilities, thrilled to be able at last to turn plans into tangible action. Buoyed by both the birth of our first child and the gratitude that came with finding somewhere so very beautiful to live, I experienced such a surge of energy that my feet hardly touched the ground. Mentally speaking, one thought tumbled into another, ideas bounced back and forth between the walls of what felt like an increasingly elastic brain. I felt stretched, but happily so. It all seemed to have such purpose; every loose strand connected to something else, each action related to the next, the goal of getting the glampsite up and running always at the centre of the wheel.

The loss of momentum that I experienced as the cows took over could have led to all sorts of mumbled gripes and groans. We'd already invested a significant part of our savings in the glamping project and had been so sure of its success that we didn't have a Plan B and therefore nothing to fall back on if things with the yurts didn't work out. When Diana would ask me what we were going to do, I really had nothing to share. What could I say? By the start of summer in 2015, the whole project was dissolving in front of our very eyes and all I wanted to do was go and sit with the cows, which is exactly what I did.

They enchanted me, made all the fuss about the glamping seem like nothing more than so much hot air and reminded me in no uncertain terms what the real project was all about. It's not that I experienced another eureka moment, nor any burning sense of epiphany, but what came in their presence, cool and deeply quiet, reignited a fire inside me that had burned itself down to the embers. The warmth that welled up in my stomach whenever I was with them was the stirring of something forgotten yet deeply familiar – the enquiry into who I was, that timeless question of all questions. One look into their shining eyes was enough to tell me all I needed to know. What I saw there, reflected in those inky deep pools, was that meditation, mindfulness, breath and self-awareness were essential to the living of a happy wholesome life and, more than that, to the flowering of the very heart itself, the pinnacle and sole aim of all human existence, whether we know it or not.

The depth of their guidance, the quiet insistence every time I went to sit with them, was startling at first. Startling yet so very subtle, almost imperceptibly so, but little by little, as June melted away into a scorchingly hot July, I realised that being mindful went hand in hand with being in their company, was something they effortlessly encouraged and supported through the living of their natural lives. And that's how it really began, the understanding that I was simply *being* with cows.

I liked the phrase immediately. It sounded full and free of complication. *Being* might mean many things to many people; in the presence of the cows, it meant nothing but quietness, a rare and deeply refreshing simplicity in which thinking was more or less totally absent. I never forgot where I was, retaining as I did full awareness of the environment around me, but the gaps between each thought would become bigger and bigger until several minutes could pass in which the mind seemed completely still, untouched by mental activity. What a relief, if but for a few moments, to be free of that incessant restless buzzing, the signature tune of thought and all its fidgety attempts to fill every second of every waking hour with its noise.

During those blistering days, evening was often the best time to be around them. As the sun dipped down behind the hills, there came in its wake a most wonderful sense of mellowness, all amber and molten gold. The forest would fill with birdsong and down through the trees would come deer, picking their way so delicately that I couldn't help but smile. What a privilege to be in such company.

On occasion, lulled by such softness into a state of quiet contemplation, I would reminisce, revisiting scene after scene of the journey that had brought me to the Pyrenees, particularly the moments that had seemed charged with a great intensity. Over the course of several such evenings, one thing became achingly clear: wherever I had been, whatever I had gotten myself involved in, there, lurking just below an oft forgotten surface, was the undeniable presence of nature. It was the one constant in my search for self-discovery, the quest to find out who I really was beyond the reach of thought and all emotion. It seemed that the yoga classes, the shamanic workshops in Scotland and the mass of other weird and wonderful things that I'd dipped my toes into served only to plunge me ever deeper into her open arms.

From my late teens on, anything green had always been good; from forests to fields and squelching bogs to mountains and moody moorland, nature had been both a best friend and ever-trusted refuge. In cities, where I sometimes experienced moments of panic, the rabbit unhinged by the glare of urban headlights would bolt to the nearest park and all would be well.

Every single path I went down, however much it twisted and turned back on itself, always without fail led me somehow back into her midst. Teachings and techniques I followed in hope of finding harmony hardly seemed to ripple the surface. Yes, there was such joy and even ecstasy at times, but nothing came close to the experience of just sitting quietly in nature. That the birds can beat thoughts and thinking into such graceful submission remains a source of wonder to this day. I mean just listen to them, the blackbird singing the day into being and little jenny wren in full flow, fairly charming the leaves off the trees with the sweetness of her song.

The heart of nature is meditation and by this I mean that singular, all-inclusive happiness that lies at the very centre of our core and being. A quote I found from Mother Teresa seemed to sum things up quite perfectly: 'God is the friend of silence. See how nature – trees, flowers, grass – grows in silence; see the stars, the moon and the sun, how they move in silence . . . We need silence to be able to touch souls.'

Sitting still for so many countless hours, sliding down those sounds of birds and gurgling streams had made this abundantly clear and now the cows were helping to bring it all back so sharply into focus.

Their own innate understanding of this, that the living of their lives was an act of meditation in itself, was proving to be deeply inspirational and began to turn going to see them into something of a spiritual practice. There were no rules to speak of, no real guidelines to follow, just an organic unfolding of something that seemed to make perfect sense. By now the Galloways were very approachable and Valentine would come of her own accord to be stroked. The Casta, however, were still decidedly standoffish, hanging back beyond some invisible barrier that they doggedly refused to cross. This was OK though. That they didn't run away at first sight of me felt like a huge step in the right direction. They were so very different from the Galloways, mysterious and always on edge. Even when Judith, the least timid of the three, would inch her way just a tiny bit closer, I began to realise that I wasn't even scratching the surface with them. I'd never come across farm animals like these before. As far as I was concerned, they were wolves in sheep's clothing, wild things merely going through the motions of domestication and I found myself becoming increasingly fascinated by what lay beneath their apparently cold exterior.

Each time I went down to see them all, I would spend the first few minutes asking them how they were doing, talking softly as I would to Gabi. I wasn't looking for any response, and it was often the case that they completely ignored me, especially the Casta, but through those quiet words, I was somehow preparing myself to be with them. It didn't matter what was said; what was important was the tone of voice and, in particular, the vibration that would gently resonate throughout the whole of my upper body. At this point, in what became the practice, I would often experience a sense of having fallen into myself, tumbling down into a quietness that brought the talking to a close. And so silenced, the real being with them would begin. It was as simple as that, whether sitting, standing or lying down on the grass. The sensation of slowing everything right down to absolute zero speed had a paralysing effect on me, so much so that at times I felt rooted to the spot.

But how to describe those moments that followed, when thinking had ground to a halt and even the sense of being a *someone* had just clean disappeared into the air? Perhaps it's best left at that – a mystery that cannot be known individually but only lived as an indivisible whole? For example, with what words could I convey the sense that the background sound of birdsong was sometimes experienced as being *inside* my body and not out there in the forest at all, or that the cows were not mere animals moving across the land but founts of immeasurable depth and wisdom?

At the time it didn't matter. Our social life was virtually non-existent, cocooned as we were on the farm, and apart from the odd volunteer or two who came to help us, it was just Diana, Gabi and me. While she didn't really have any natural interest in the cows, Diana could sense something was going on with them but never for a moment was I pressed to share what it might be. It meant I was free to leave the experiences exactly as I found them. No attempt was made to try to squeeze them into words, to dilute them with explanation or milk them for profit or pleasure.

The sessions normally came to a kind of natural end when the cows casually ambled off to another part of the meadow to graze. Even, as was the case on several occasions, they wandered off as soon as I arrived at their side, I would thank them for their company, for their generosity, and slowly take my leave. The sessions had absolutely nothing to do with time; ten minutes could be ten hours, or the briefest glance a whole week's worth of workshops. And when I say ended, I say so in jest, for how could such seamless flashings of perfection be brought to any end at all? This became increasingly obvious the more I went to see them. It's not that the quietness and sense of simply being came to a halt when I left, more that the habitual thoughts and daydreams washed right back in, tumbling me over and over until at times I forgot that such peace could even exist. That silence is always here, they would remind me, but it's your job to remember it, that's all.

Sometimes great effort is needed to achieve something of value or importance in one's life but what was happening with the cows was the epitome of effortlessness. What came with them was unlooked for. I hadn't consciously desired it nor read anything about such things before. I knew that I was far from the first to encounter such life-changing experiences with cattle – a whole devotional mass of poems and Hindu scripture is full of it – and that I wouldn't be the last to find such shelter at their side, but what moved me was the fact that it all appeared to be happening so organically, like a seed that had finally found its natural earth.

For as long as I could remember, spontaneity had been a powerful force in my life. I'm sure if I tried to retrace my footsteps, the route would be characterised by sudden twists and turns that appeared to make no logical sense. I felt naturally aligned with these organic, out-of-the-blue occurrences, things that simply popped up without prior thought or planning. I loved the idea that Life could manifest something wherever and whenever it wanted to, according to its own unknown agenda. To be spontaneous was to hear its natural language, to be alive to its movement and its wishes, unfathomable as they may have been to my thinking mind.

# CHAPTER 4

# The Maharshi

'A Guru need not always be in human form.'

RAMANA MAHARSHI

By late August of that year, the heat was beginning to become more bearable and I was sitting with Gabi and the cows late one afternoon when my thoughts began to settle on this theme of spur-of-the-moment happenings. I was thinking about how in one sense, everything that happened in life could be said to be something of a spontaneous occurrence, even the most mundane lifting of a finger to scratch one's nose, when into my mind popped an image of Ramana Maharshi. Shortly before we bought the farm I had been introduced to this most revered of modern-day Indian saints by a close friend, and from the very first moment I had been deeply moved by the sheer simplicity of his words. Prior to this, I'd never taken any interest in anything to do with Indian philosophy, religion or spiritual practice. Yes, there had been yoga, but the classes I took had been focused almost exclusively on the physical aspect, with very little if any instruction regarding meditation or spiritual practice. In a way that I cannot explain, I felt, on discovering his teachings, that at very long last I had come home to myself. And sitting there with his image flickering in and out of my thoughts, I remembered having read that his moment of self-realisation, the ending of his apparent existence as an individually separate entity, had also been an out-of-the-blue event, albeit one of an unimaginable intensity.

In 1896, he had been sitting in his room at home when he was suddenly gripped by a terrifying fear of dying. There had been no warning, no trembling of his earth to indicate the landslide to come, not in the days leading up to the event, nor throughout his childhood or early teenage years.

In his own words,

'The shock of fear of death made me at once intro-spective, or "introverted". I said to myself mentally, i.e., without uttering the words – "Now, death has come. What does it mean? What is it that is dying? This body dies."

I at once dramatised the scene of death. I extended my limbs and held them rigid as though rigor-mortis had set in. I imitated a corpse to lend an air of reality to my further investigation; I held my breath and kept my mouth closed, pressing the lips tightly together so that no sound might escape. Let not the word "I" or any other word be uttered!

"Well then," said I to myself, "this body is dead. It will be carried stiff to the burning ground and there burnt and reduced to ashes. But with the death of this body, am 'I' dead? Is the body 'I'? This body is silent and inert. But I feel the full force of my personality and even the sound 'I' within myself – apart from the body. So 'I' am a spirit, a thing transcending the body. The material body dies, but the spirit transcending it cannot be touched by death. I am therefore the deathless spirit.'"[1]

The discovery of the Maharshi's work was essential in so many nameless ways; I instinctively knew that it signified the end of the game, the final whistle, the curtain call on endless attempts to even find the beginning of a thread. I can't say how but something was telling me that this thread, once grasped and followed, would lead me back to the home that I'd never left in the first place, contrary to what my thoughts would be constantly telling me. And crucially, it laid the foundations upon which all that was happening with the cows could be built. It dawned on me during those late-summer days that his words made most sense when I was with them, for the unwaveringly reliable peace to be found in their presence worked as a kind of interface between the teachings and my restless mind.

I took to reading his teachings in their company, aloud at times so that the cows could also partake in the sweetness that I felt had been gifted to me in the form of his work. I'd been doing this for a week or two, whenever I had the chance, even feeling a little smug that the cows could be benefitting in some way from the sessions, when

1 Narasimha Swami, B Vx, *Self Realisation*

Jalie delivered a very stark reminder of the importance of humility to those who are earnestly seeking the seat of their own existence.

I'd only been with the cows for a few minutes, enough to find a comfy spot in the shade of a huge old poplar, when she left the group and walked very purposefully over towards me. I only just had time to grab the book that lay on the grass beside me before she quite literally chased me out of the meadow. I had tried to make a stand and let her know that all was well, but from the depths of her innate Casta-certified allegiance to honesty, she was having none of it.

When I stood staring into her unblinking eyes from the other side of the fence, she seemed to be challenging me somehow, calling my bluff in a way that I'd never experienced before. I couldn't say that she was being obviously aggressive or threatening in a physical sense, yet through her spotless eyes she was telling me to simply drop all the bullshit, the stuff about reading to her and the rest of the cows as if *I* was the one in the know. Drop it Dave, she said, just let it go.

How does it feel to be belittled by a two-year-old still-skinny sack of horn and bristling defiance? Pretty dodgy at first, actually. I felt suddenly confronted by a sense of deceit-fulness, of having been such a blatant fraud in front of the very beings that were repeatedly telling me of the need to stay quiet and mindful. The Lord's Prayer and its deliverance from evil may be interpreted in a million different ways, yet with Jalie standing guard over my shattered sense of pride, it was seen as a plea to be free from temptation and the constant succumbing to thoughts. Yes, through thinking that *I* was the one to bring the Maharshi to the cows, I had also in some way given in to temptation. *Lead me not* is just one way of saying 'help me to stay mindful and aware of all that mental traffic', a wish to stay detached and simply observant of all that thinking appears to bring.

When the rest of the herd ambled over to stand with Jalie, I tried to apologise, but the look on their faces made a mockery of any desire to do so. You fool, I said to myself and then, to the cows, you already know, don't you? It was a masterclass in non-violent (just!), mindful acceptance of the limiting nature of thought. The biter was bit, the salesman sold down the river of his own ignorant making. Doing nothing but remaining true to their natural sense of what is right, the cows had delivered a lesson that remains with me to this very day. 'You lot,' I shouted, out as I walked back to the chalet.

Later that evening, as I was sharing the experience with Diana, it dawned on me that the appearance of both the Saint and the cows in my life and their apparent compatibility was beyond the reach of any speculative sense of coincidence. They came as part of the same package, a programme constantly refined and updated according to unknown workings of the heart. It seemed perfectly natural and even obvious that they should go hand in hand, if that's what Life itself had decided. Who was I to question their origins or seek explanation for their presence in what was increasingly seen as a fiction of a life? I just couldn't operate like that anymore.

Among the mass of sayings and material that has been

attributed to the Maharshi, there is one short, sharp phrase that is undeniably accepted as being the very essence and undiluted well-spring of his teachings – the question 'Who Am I?' The practice of Self-Enquiry invites questioning to whom all experiences occur. It demands that the enquirer meets each and every thought with an immediate investigation pertaining to its origin. By tracing all mental activity back to its source, the serious and committed devotee, determined and desiring nothing else, can earn liberation. Being with the cows slowed the normally raging torrent of thoughts right down to a trickle and this made it possible to put self-enquiry into practice, really going deeply into it, in a more solid and concrete way. Living quietly, mindfully, was their daily bread and butter. The cows were well cared-for, loved, and they lived in the midst of a most beautifully hobbit-like patchwork of hills and wooded valleys, and the combination of all these apparent elements made meditation an automatic response to seeing them. I couldn't help but become quiet around them.

One story, in particular, that I read during that period became a guiding light, a confirmation that whatever was happening with the Galloways and Casta was quite clearly something of the heart. It brought with it, at times, a tingling sensation of inspiration, a great green light to continue deep diving down into uncharted depths. In brief, it recounted the relationship between the Maharshi and a cow called Lakshmi, who although wrapped up in animal form, became his most ardent and unwavering devotee. It is reported than on her deathbed, she achieved liberation under the watchful gaze and touch of the saint, whose tears, mourning the loss of a dear and unearthly friend, confirmed for all those in attendance the unique place that she had found in his heart.

Reading such accounts was like the relighting of a touch paper that was already well ablaze, and the fire was all-consuming. I began to look at the cows in an even more revelatory light, feeling at times that I was truly in the presence of so many cloven-hoofed masters. To think of myself as anything but their humble servant seemed ridiculous, and this growing sense of their sacredness immediately ended any idea whatsoever that any of them would ever be sent to the slaughterhouse. This had never been part of the plan anyway, loose-limbed as it was, but by now it had become an immovable impossibility. Route definitely and permanently *barrée*.

One evening in late September, I had an experience that summed up everything they had inspired in me over the course of the long hot summer. Perhaps, in light of the deeply disturbing upheavals that were soon to follow, it was Life's way of anchoring me ever deeper into the practice of self-enquiry, providing me most compassionately with the means to deal with such a devastating blow.

I'd found the cows grazing steadily together in one of the hilltop meadows. They always climbed up to the highest parts of the land at the end of the day. It was fresher up there, more likely to catch any breeze blowing down the valley, and sometimes I felt that they also liked the view, a spectacular span of Pyrenean splendour piled up against the skyline. After greeting them in the normal way, I sat down to enjoy the whole idyllic scene. Entering into the familiar sense of completeness that came in their company, I lost myself for a while in watching countless swallows and martins carving the sky into so many little pieces. They were gathering in ever-increasing numbers, gorging themselves ahead of their journey south, heroes every one of them. Some of them came swooping down to ground level, skimming the grass at breakneck speed, feasting on flies and other winged insects. To see them swerving so gracefully between the cows brought a smile to my face. 'What a joy to see such things,' I thought.

By now, the warmth that was beginning to bubble up from my belly had lulled me into a very deep sense of relaxation. Everything felt perfectly still, including the flight of the swallows and the breeze ruffling the treetops. A great lethargy washed over me and, closing my eyes, I fell into a deep sleep. On awaking sometime later there before me sat the cows, all placidly chewing the cud. Such a thing had never happened before in their presence. I was delighted at first, thrilled that they felt confident enough to come so close, particularly the Casta. Judith, in fact, was not a metre away, near enough for her sweet-smelling breath to be a perfume of sorts in the air. I couldn't resist and reached out to touch her nose and it was then, right at the moment I felt her soft fur beneath my fingers for the very first time, that *the* question resurfaced, leaping up from the depths to demand *who am I?* In a flash, a millisecond perhaps of tick-tock time, I knew what it might really mean to be whole. Just being. All sense of individuality evaporated. The question was not meant to have an answer; its true and everlasting beauty lay in the fact that it was designed to dismantle the questioner. This was the Maharshi's secret weapon, the absolute essence of his ABC. I laughed out loud, and it felt like the cows were laughing too; everything, in fact, was tittering away in tones of glee – the trees, the clouds and even an old jay perched high above me, its rasping call included. The initial delight had given way to bliss, and when even that had laughed itself out, what remained can only be spoken about in terms of *absence*, for it felt like all I had ever considered myself to be had, in one blink of an unseeing eye, been struck from the face of the earth. No longer known at my home address, there was only that *current* that the Maharshi had spoken of during his sudden awakening as a youth. For the briefest of moments, there was perfect clarity.

When I left the cows to it, slowly winding my way down through the woodland, the thoughts were already at it again, yet somehow more distant now, less invasive or able to distract. It remained that way for the best part of a month. I felt changed. A subtle difference in my experience of everyday life meant that thoughts could come and go more fluidly. It didn't seem to matter if I got stuck for a while, having wandered off into one daydream or another, for as soon as I saw the cows or remembered the *current*, all was well in a mindful sort of way.

And this, as I was soon to tragically discover, was the preparation, Life's great compassion in action. It was an integral part of the trauma lurking just around the corner and when the walls did come tumbling down, block after unbearable block, I was able to stand firmly on the foundations that the whole experience had uncovered.

# CHAPTER 5

# From tears to transformation

'What a caterpillar calls the end of the world the master calls a butterfly.'

RICHARD BACH

Autumn in Mirepoix is often a most beautiful time of year and it was no different in 2015. The intense heat of summer had long since passed and now was a time to enjoy the gentle warmth that late October often brings to this part of south-western France. Early morning had seen mist lying softly upon the valley floor but now only a few scattered wisps remained. The Pyrenees, reaching high above the wooded hills at the end of the valley, were looking their magnificent best. Already snow-capped at the peaks, they leant a certain solidity to the whole dream-like scene.

The morning had been spent at the local market. Boasting one of the most well-preserved mediaeval squares in the whole region, Mirepoix hosts a market befitting of its picture-postcard good looks. A mass of colourful stalls pack themselves in, straining under the weight of cheeses, wine and smoke-cured sides of ham. What's most pleasing of all is the sheer number of organic producers crammed into the side-streets and alleys. Fruits and vegetables of the season, still covered in the soil in which they grew, mountain honey that's more medicine than food, and an assortment of artisan-made arts and crafts all testify to the health and vibrancy of the local organic movement.

In the afternoon, along with Eryc and Mara, the two volunteers who were staying with us on the farm at the time, we began to clean up a large patch of briars and brambles that had taken over part of one of the streamside meadows.

How quickly they grow in this climate, anchored by roots that delve deep in search of water. Brambles are stubborn things. They don't give in easily. They are survivors who just keep coming back. Chop them down and they only grow stronger. I couldn't help but respect them and their refusal to just lie down and die. I'd even named one our dogs after them.

Returning to the wooden chalet, preparations began for the evening meal. Diana was playing with Gabi, and Eryc and Mara were helping me out with supper. There was a tangible sense of wellbeing in the air, a feeling of fullness and satisfaction at having done a good afternoon's work. The crickets were still managing the odd chirp or two in the nearby meadows and down from the wooded hillsides tumbled the twit-twooing of tawny owls. They are always so vocal at that time of year when the adolescent young, squawking and screeching, are driven from their parents' territories.

When the phone rang and I picked it up, I was happy to hear the sound of Dad's voice.

'Hi, Dave.'

'Donald . . . how be thee?'

'Dave,' he said, 'I've got some devastating news. Cork has committed suicide. He was found in a patch of woodland up by the village. Shot himself in the head. He'd stolen a pistol from the kennels.'

I don't remember the rest of the conversation.

At first came fear, a shock that sat as a solid ball pressing hard in the centre of the chest. I struggled to breathe for a moment as the pressure squeezed its way up and around the heart. Then came panic and a desire to flee. The head said get up and run, but I knew the legs wouldn't carry me. In the same unbearable moment, there emerged from my mouth a phrase, repeated over and over: 'He's free now, he's free.' It seemed to climb and soar and weave in and out of the unheard words that Dad was weeping down the phone.

When I realised that he had stopped speaking and Mum had taken his place, it seemed that the air became charged with an almost crushing sense of raw power. Everything simply stopped in the way things do before the coming of a great thunderstorm. Her voice was so calm and still, such a shocking bottomless pool of loss and maternal longing. I'd never heard Mum speak in that way before, with such a tone of impossible quietude. He was my brother, but she was the mother hen in mourning for one of her brood.

As she continued to talk and sigh from God knows

what depths of despair, there was a sense of having been split into several pieces. One part listened, others were occupied with feelings and thoughts and yet another, the clearest of all, sat above the rest in quiet detachment. Unruffled, it seemed, and untouched by the staggering sense of seeing a world just crumble around me.

And then the storm broke and with it came tears of the like I'd never cried before.

And I cried and cried and cried.

An evening of gentle contentment had dissolved in the blink of an eye. A five-minute phone-call had turned heaven into hell. Eryc's face, which moments before had been all shiny with smiles, had become a picture of perfect loss. He didn't even know my brother.

I rang Pete, my older brother, but we couldn't speak. What could we say? I could tell he was shattered into so many awful pieces.

I turned to Diana and at first it seemed as if she couldn't understand what had happened, refused to believe what, between sobs, I was trying to tell her. 'He's dead . . . my brother is dead! Cork. He's gone.'

Gabi sat proudly on his potty, his gurgling little laugh a lifeline of sorts that brought me softly to my knees. I clung to the sound of his sing-song voice as one might the rail of a storm-battered ship. He was my only link with normality, the only solid ground in a world suddenly flooded with pain.

I picked up the laptop, opened YouTube and as if on automatic pilot found The Hollies song 'He ain't heavy, he's my brother.' Over and over the song was played, dredging deeper and deeper down into a thick bed of grief.

And there I sat, wallowing in a muddy mix of pain and utter loneliness.

At times Cork's face seemed to hover in front of me, out of reach and untouchable. It didn't feel like a dream – as some have reported – and I knew without doubt he had gone, never to return in the form that we'd all adored. Many people who have had near-death experiences often report that while dead, they were shown an incredibly detailed review of their life. It wasn't me who had died, but for several minutes a stream of memories flooded my vision. Cork as a baby, a blond-haired angel of a boy, teenage mud fights and nights spent sitting up trees on badger watch. All went flashing by. I remembered his eyes in particular, that sparkle which had brought Mum and many of the older aunties to call him their little sunshine boy. And I remembered the dimming of that light, the putting up of shutters till it shone no more and I started crying all over again.

Mara came for a moment and wrapped her arms around my shoulders. There was gratitude for the gesture, yet a numbing sense of separation made a barrier to such acts of genuine kindness and compassion. There was nothing she could do.

As darkness fell and the hooting of the owls echoed back and forth along the valley, I remembered that Cork was meant to have been coming to see us in two days' time, flying out with Mum and his two kids, Henry and Jessie, to spend a few days on the farm. I'd been looking forward to it so very much. I still missed my family, even though I'd been in France for over two years already, and the idea of having the great fool of a brother himself come to stay had filled me with a bubbling sense of excitement. When we'd spoken on the phone in the weeks and days leading up to the visit, I knew that he'd been struggling again with his moods. However, he'd been to see a counsellor, which was a first for him, and at the time I felt that he might just be beginning to turn a corner and get to grips with what was really troubling him deep down.

So near and yet so very, very far . . .

Later in the evening came a sense of calm. Holding a sleeping Gabi in my arms, the tears dried up and a quietness seemed to cocoon itself around me. The beloved Corky I had known and almost worshipped had gone. There was nothing to be questioned or analysed, no need for reflection on what could have been and nothing to do but try sit in the acceptance of it all.

Not for a moment was there any sense of nonacceptance, of denying the death of my brother, nor any thought about the how and why and what for. The expression of loss through the tears had been total. Crying is how your heart speaks when your words can't explain the pain you feel.

As a leaf falls from a tree in autumn and a dewdrop dries and disappears in the warmth of the morning sunshine, so my beloved brother had left the stage behind him. I knew he no longer existed as he had and also knew, instinctively, that memory could offer at best poor and tasteless crumbs of comfort.

Perhaps I was blessed to have been given such acceptance so quickly? Perhaps it was this that brought such uncalled-for quietness, that cocoon of something calm and soothing in the midst of the pain and the grief? Yes, of course there was devastation, a sickly sense of loss that had set up camp in the stomach, yet not for a single moment came disbelief or any notion of unreality. That he had gone was undeniable and acknowledgement of this brought some kind of stillness into the candle-lit air of the chalet.

As Beith, one of our dogs, curled up on my lap, her presence deepened this strange sense of having been soothed by some unknown source of comfort. Cork had lived for his dogs, terriers mostly, and Beith's presence brought tears again. She licked them from my face and in so doing, wiped away any lingering trace of denial. Gazing into her soothing eyes, soft with devotion as always, she seemed to say that all was well, despite my feeling of having been torn in two.

It was then that I realised that I couldn't hold on to memories of Cork as he had once appeared, for it felt as if such an action was based upon my desire to have things different to how Life had actually made them. In the brief moments of such clarity, when the grief became simply a part of the whole, rather than a crushing weight of isolation, I felt that I could feel Cork flying free, unzipped and, excuse the pun, uncorked.

Any grief and pain that I continued to cling to was more a reflection of my own suffering. I began to ask myself what seemed at the time a strange and even selfish question: 'For whom am I grieving and who has been lost?' No answer was necessary. The importance was in the questioning of the pain. Who is it that grieves? To whom does the grieving occur? Something compelled me to keep digging in, right down into the very seat of the pain itself.

This is not to say that to grieve is either wrong or right, for this is really not the point. It was simply a spontaneously occurring enquiry in the midst of a heart-breakingly sad upheaval. To question the origin of pain or trauma, grief, sadness or any other thought or emotion, is to go straight to the heart of the matter. It isn't concerned with the feeling or thought itself, but with from where it comes and who it occurs to.

When Beith went to lie down in her basket later that night, my eyes came to rest on the photo that was pinned to the wall of the chalet. It was the Maharshi. His only written teaching guide was originally traced with his finger into sand. Sometime in the 1920s, it became an essay, written in a question-and-answer format. It was called, quite simply, 'Who am I?'

The essay began with the following paragraph:

'Every living being longs to be perpetually happy, without any misery. Since in everyone the highest love is alone felt for oneself, and since happiness alone is the cause of love, in order to attain that happiness, which is one's real nature and which is experienced daily in the mindless state of deep sleep, it is necessary to know oneself. To achieve that, enquiry in the form "Who am I?" is the foremost means.'

My brother *was* in misery. A big black pit of a hole, that slowly but surely swallowed him. A near impossibly beautiful face made bloated and blotched by endless packets of antidepressants as he tried desperately to bluff his way through life. His powerful, athletic body became flabby. He felt so intensely alone, so separate and utterly unreachable, that almost every hour of every waking day was spent in the midst of an unceasing nightmare.

Alcohol and tablets are rarely a mixture that leads to healing and stability. Corky's clutching-at-straws dependency on the two reflected the depth of the gaping wound that pained him so.

He became a supreme actor, the star of his very own tragi-comedy, in which the happy fool, so loved by all who knew him, played on till the very end. Outside shiny; inside shot to pieces: the jovial cheeky charmer who hid his pain behind smiles and witty one-liners.

When, a couple of days later, I rang a close friend to tell him that Cork had taken his own life, he told me that in his opinion it was an act of non-acceptance, that in effect my brother was, in a most extreme way, running away from himself and the things that troubled him so very much.

Opinions! Who cares for them? I put the phone down boiling with anger. Tears welled up again, and then the thought of the courage it must take to point a gun to your head and actually pull the trigger. That moment:

that step into a total unknown, leaving everything and everyone behind . . . kids, wife, dogs, family and friends. It must take balls, mustn't it? You'd have to be strong to choose to go through with something that for many is difficult to even talk about.

At the most basic and fundamental level, Cork, too, simply wished to be happy. Shooting himself in the head was, for him, the most appropriate means of achieving this end, even if it could, by some, be perceived as a running away from his unrelenting pain.

His sensitivity allowed him no barriers behind which he could hide. No refuge existed for one who had reached the limit of his personal existence. The safety he so desperately sought, and the love he craved and died for, eluded him right up to the moment that the trigger was finally squeezed.

All suffering exists through identification with the personal; the idea that Corky's extreme state of anxiety indicated a refusal from somewhere deep inside him to continue to play its game. He saw behind its façade, knew that the body and world were but images flickering to and fro on an oft-forgotten screen.

One look in his shining eyes would tell you this. And he simply grew tired of it all.

As a child he was loved beyond measure. The youngest of three sons and an adored brother, we fairly worshipped him, our little sunshine boy. He was held in such awe by us all that it genuinely seemed as if we had an angel in our midst. It's so very easy, perhaps, to look back through rose-tinted specs, to see only good things to cling to, yet in Corky's case, certainly throughout his childhood and even adolescent years, he was characterised by an innocence and an almost heart-breaking sense of naivety that touched many who crossed his path. He was a blonde, gap-toothed gift from God, who lit up our days with such light and natural warmth.

From such a safe and calm beginning, it's perhaps not difficult to understand that in later years, when the skies darkened, he simply didn't know how to cope with the thunder and lightning and rain.

Home had been such a strong shelter that it seems he was somehow defenceless outside its solid walls. The almost achingly pure sense of innocence that he carried right through, even until his early teenage years, made him so vulnerable to the rough and tumble of life outside the familiar nest, that when the first waves of doubt crashed down upon his shore, he struggled to keep his head above the surf.

As I watched him slowly descend over several years into a shadow of his former self, I knew he was aware of his own plight, of the tightrope he walked and that one day he would simply slip and fall away.

Almost until the very end, he refused all offers of help. The proverbial clam kept its shell so tightly shut that not even his closest friends and family were granted access to his innermost thoughts and feelings.

At times, it felt as if I could see him being eaten alive by the forces that twisted and ripped him to pieces. If anyone tried to get close to him, to ask how he might be feeling, to question the dependence on antidepressants, he would vanish as if in a puff of smoke. He wriggled his way out of every question, shunned attempts to shine a light into those darkest nooks and crannies and evaded invitations to talk or even just go for a walk together.

By God he tried in his own way to keep on keeping on, but in the end, his demons devoured him.

At his funeral, I had wanted to carry his coffin into the church, along with my other brother Pete and several of Cork's closest friends, but when the hearse arrived, my legs buckled beneath me. In that difficult moment, all acceptance of what had happened, the mindful recognition that death was but another part of Life, seemed to count for absolutely nothing. At first, I grabbed hold of someone, desperate for support and then I ran away. Straight through the hundreds of startled mourners, head down, jelly-legged, to stand by the side of his waiting grave. Squatting down, I reached out to the soft November earth. Worcestershire Clay. A great big pile of it. It felt good in the hand, something I could trust and cling to. I rolled it into little balls and threw them, one after another, into the grave. For a minute, I felt so ashamed that I'd fallen so foul of fear, but talking to Cork made it easier to breathe and I asked him to forgive me. When a little robin landed on the bough of an oak overlooking the grave, he felt so close at hand it seemed as if he had delivered his answer personally. Neither of us moved for a while and then, when his work was done, he flew away as suddenly as he'd arrived.

Walking back into the church was easier after that.

When Cork was lowered gently into the grave, I could

see that Mum and Dad were sinking down with him, some part of them buried forever. So many around were weeping and I cried too, but the tears were for my parents, not Cork. What strength I saw, what courage and capacity to bear the unbearable so graciously. I could never dare to imagine how they were feeling. My mum's eyes spoke of something beyond words, a place beyond pain even, that had no need of name. Dad, upright and unblinking, faced the day with enduring poise, the epitome of kindness and goodwill to all who'd come to pay their respects, but later that evening, slumped in a chair at home, he was crushed by the weight of grief. When I sat down next to him, he took my hand in his and for the first time I could remember in our lives, asked silently for support.

Parting from my family after the funeral was incredibly difficult. I hadn't wanted to leave and felt so guilty doing so. Being at home provided sanctuary of a sort. Cocooned from the outside world, Mum, myself and Pete often spent hours walking the footpaths and fields, nosing through woodland with the dogs, doing the things that we'd always done and which Cork had loved doing too. Walking was in our blood: it nourished us, enriched us and constantly cemented our bond with the natural world around us. In the aftermath of Cork's death, it carried us through the dark November days when the gloom of grey-washed skies reflected the colour of our grief and sense of loss.

Pain can bring its own form of quietness and, during

those days, we did little but eat, sleep and walk, calmly and quietly going about our business. For several weeks, life became simplicity itself. The grief, like some great unyielding axe, cleaved straight through the parts of our lives that at the time seemed surplus to requirements. It was as if the rest of the world just ceased to exist. As a family, we turned inward, looking first to ourselves for support and then to the countryside around us. This was how we managed and while we were all together, it worked.

The worst part, when we left, was saying goodbye to Henry and Jessie, Cork's two young kids. I felt that his wife, Rhian, devastated as she was, had an inner strength that would see her through the desperate days to come, but I near enough drowned in the tears that the little ones shed as we parted, an unstoppable flow that left a gaping hole in my stomach. I felt gutted. During the first hours on the way back to France, I felt as if I'd abandoned them, all of them, the whole family. Gabi gave shelter from the storm and I clung to him as if shipwrecked, yet still at sea.

It was the cows who led me unknowingly into full acceptance. I say unknowingly because what followed with them was yet another example of their capacity to amaze, to reveal yet more layers of depth and humility. The bond with them, the role they played in my universe as teachers and guides, was already well established, yet nothing could have prepared me for the compassion and sense of pure refuge that I was about to experience in their presence.

It started just hours after arriving back on the farm.

# From tears to transformation

Those first moments back in Mirepoix were some of the loneliest I can ever remember. In our absence, the woodland trees had shed their leaves and their stark scratchy outlines offered no sense of comfort at all. It had still been warm and sunny when we had left for England. Now, blankets of cold grey cloud smothered the mountains. It was as if someone had pulled an unseen plug and all the living colour had drained away and out of the world.

The coats of both the Casta and Galloway grow longer in autumn and winter. The Casta are covered in a thick layer of fur, not too unlike that of the red and roe deer with whom they shared the farm. With the Galloways it's more like wool, finer and softer to the touch. For both, their colours are muted: the deep chestnut brown of the Casta and black or dun of the Galloways.

However, when I saw them again in that watery afternoon light, it seemed like they shone with all the colours of the rainbow. Straight through those layers of pain they came, bucking and bouncing at the sound of my voice. They fairly exploded out of the trees, careering down the scrubby slope towards where I stood at the bottom of the valley. Smiling for the first time since Cork's death, I realised just how very much I had missed them and their unassuming presence. Valentine in particular gave me such a deep and knowing look that for several minutes I wept uncontrollably, wetting her nose with my tears. The rest of them stood quietly around me, the Casta calm in a way that I'd never seen before. Even Jalie, the most restless and suspiciously distant of them all, expressed a depth of compassion that I hadn't thought her capable of. I could see it in her eyes and feel from the way she stood so quiet and still that somehow she understood.

For however long I stayed there, all the pain from the previous weeks of upheaval slipped right off the screen.

So all-encompassing was the cows' attention that I barely felt or thought anything. The homesickness, the grief and that aching sense of loneliness just fell away. I wasn't even aware of what was happening at the time, so total was the absence of self-consciousness. It was only when I turned to go and the pain started sloshing around again that I realised something had happened, that there had been a break in its bottomless flow.

It was a crucial shift, the beginning of something so unimaginable that I can only attribute it to Life's endless ability to express an unthinkable depth of compassion. How else can I explain that aching sense of understanding that I experienced coming from the cows during those first few minutes back together? They knew what had happened in some unknowable way and their response was beautiful beyond description.

From that moment on they never failed me. All throughout the rest of autumn and into the beginning of 2016, they carried me on their backs, leaving me somewhere each evening that was better than the day before. All the normal day-to-day activities involved in looking after them – the feeding, the topping up of water troughs, running up fence lines and the like – were automatically and often completely unconsciously converted into opportunities firstly just to breathe deeply and slowly and then, into moments of quite raw and undiluted acceptance. Cork was almost constantly on my mind, yet the cows made being with his loss less sickening. The queasiness that constantly tumbled around in my stomach during those days was almost instantly soothed by the lick of a rasping tongue or the buffeting I regularly received from so many furry heads all jostling for position. Even their smell came to be a powerful tonic of sorts. It represented honesty, warmth and an ability to endure, something so earthy that it could carry the weight of its own world on its shoulders.

By the time spring announced its arrival in the songs of birds filling the woodland, most of the pain had fallen away. Tears still came and that was perfectly OK, as did memories from childhood of playing with the great fool himself – endless games of football and tag and bike rides to the end of our world and back, but whenever I was with them, the cows, I didn't think of Cork, of Henry and Jessie or anyone else. In fact, I rarely thought at all. Their gift was in deepening the ability to be mindful, bringing me gently, imperceptibly into the present moment. The being with cows, boosted in a strange and difficult way by the circumstances of the previous months, just got deeper and deeper.

Judith and Valentine, being the dominant females of the Casta and Galloways, took the lead in this immersive process, signalling quite openly their availability and willingness to spend more time together. At first, this took the form of approaching me directly as soon as I entered their presence or, following quietly behind as I took my leave, accompanying me back to the gate or gap in the hedge. It genuinely felt as if they were looking out for me, had taken me under their collective wing. At times, with one on my left and the other on my right, it felt as if they had become armbands of sorts, two living, breathing buoyancy aids whose gentle presence helped keep my head above the still difficult waters. I could even say that they were in some way mothering me. Neither of them had yet calved, but the care and concern they so regularly displayed seemed so deeply maternal and loving.

Judith, in particular, even with her fine set of black-tipped horns, was the most gentle and caring of all, nothing but pure and simple kindness. Hers was a less obvious approach than the rough and tumble of Valentine's sometime version of tough love, yet her mere presence provided the perfect balm to soothe those lingering wounds. One evening, as the see-saw song of chiff-chaffs and others who'd made it back safe and sound from Africa poured down from the woodland, I sat with her for a while. The rest of the herd had moved further up the field to graze and she alone remained, her head resting on the floor. This in itself was unusual as the social bonds that the cows shared between them normally meant that things were done en masse. All for one and one for all was just about the way of things, but this time, her continued presence in the corner of the field seemed, to me at least, to say that she was, on occasion, beyond such instinctive behaviour. As I looked in her eyes, shiny as ever and unfathomably deep, I couldn't see her as a cow or animal of any kind. How on earth could such a bottomless pool of being be reduced to the level of a word? It seemed that such an idea was ridiculous, an insult even to the quietness that had gently enveloped us. In those moments, she was, as she is, Life itself. Her gaze was terribly penetrating, terrible in a way only to thoughts and thinking. Otherwise, there was music and dance, a cascade of empty appreciation and absence of anything upon which thought may get a foothold. It felt as if all the juicy sap of spring was suddenly concentrated in her form, a pure expression of renewal and transformation. When she left to join the others, I was convinced that I had been in the presence of a saint or sage, one capable of bestowing on another something of the cleanest and most pristine of qualities. Oh Judith.

Mum and Dad often came to stay with us on the farm that spring of 2016, and I felt that the visits played an important part in helping all of us come to terms with the loss. We spent hours working in the woodland, clearing the brush, lighting fires, and sometimes baking our own potatoes in the embers. Spending so long among the trees did the job, of course, as they quietly wrapped their helping hands around us. We were forest-bathing every day, immersing ourselves in the greenery, breathing the clean air of a region totally devoid of heavy industry. Our undefined therapy sessions were watching red and roe deer grazing at dusk in the meadows. Nature *is* the original counselling session. No appointment is needed, no tools or techniques, even, just a willingness to sit or walk quietly in her midst. Watching a faun trot along by the side of its mother brought quietness and from it the knowledge that pain is never permanent.

Already close, we became almost nakedly honest with each other. While this was not always something pleasant to experience, it was ultimately incredibly liberating and allowed us to find a friendship that is a privilege to be a part of.

As spring gave way to an incredibly hot start to summer, I had arrived at a point of almost complete acceptance with regard to Cork and his passing. After the storm comes the calm, and the cows had brought me to a place of quiet, reliable steadiness. There was a sense of having been anchored to the earth, a firm implantation into something solid, yet soft and deeply supportive.

And as I witnessed these changes in myself, the relationship with the cows also began to transform itself into something that spoke less of dependency and more of inspiration. I still spent the same amount of time with them, often wandering for hours through the forest trying to find them, and continued to be charmed by the mere sight of them, but I was beginning to realise that I no longer *needed them* quite so much as I thought I did. The intensity of the previous months and all that they entailed meant that I'd become very deeply attached to them and had been, many times over during the darkest days, reluctant to leave their side. They were my antidepressants, counsellors, psychotherapists and guides all rolled up into one perfect bovine bundle. Outside the circle of family and friends, I never spoke to anyone about my grief, never sought any professional help or support, and never looked any further than the four-legged friends I was blessed to be with.

It was natural, then, for they themselves to usher me into a greater awareness and appreciation of what their presence on the farm might represent. When I sat with them during those days, the atmosphere in and around them began to fizz with possibility. I couldn't attribute such a feeling to the season, for the potential that comes with spring's promise of fertility was already a distant memory, nothing but dust in what had become a parched and barren landscape. At first it seemed to exist as something barely suggested, an unknown sense of change that hadn't yet taken form. It shimmered just out of reach. Physically speaking, this was often translated as a queasiness in my stomach, pleasant perhaps, like a ticklish itch, but one that no amount of scratching could relieve.

And then, one evening, Judith came and said it was all about sharing. She'd got up from her place beside an old stump, slowly walked over to where I stood, and lowered her head to be scratched. I was still revelling in this kind of contact, impossible as it had seemed at first with the Casta, and was grateful enough to simply be there, scratching away, when she suddenly began shaking her head forcibly from side to side. The Casta often do this when they are nervous or unsure of a situation, and in light of the fine set of horns she now possessed, I backed away. I was confused. Was she telling me to back off?

Had she lost her trust in me? Had I touched a sore spot on her neck, behind her ears? When she moved towards me again, head down, I did feel fear for a moment, afraid that the bond had been broken, and I instinctively moved away. As she continued to come on, I picked my way back several yards, until I came up against a large stand of brambles and blackthorn. There was no way through, and as she arrived in front of me, I put up a hand in an attempt to maintain some distance. When she started to lick it, rasping the skin with her file-rough tongue, a nervous laugh escaped me. I sniggered, then sighed, and as the adrenalin subsided, I slipped effortlessly down into a very deep peace indeed. Judith sat down beside me, staring softly into space, a statue I thought, the solid expression of calm and total quietness. It was then that I suddenly knew what I had to do, what moving to the farm was really about, regardless of all the plans and hour upon hour of discussion and at times heated debate. Clarity of such a crystalline nature cannot be questioned, and as I sat down beside Judith, closer and closer until I was able to lean back against her body, I thought firstly of Cork and then of what now had to be done by way of honouring both his life and his memory.

The Merriam-Webster dictionary lists seven definitions of the word *inspiration*, the second of which reads as 'the quality or state of being inspired.' Without doubt, the cows were proving to be nothing but inspirational and constantly capable of evoking in me that particular state. However, definition number five is more accurate, more specific and closely expressive of how I felt the cows had plodded right in and nudged their way into the very heart of my whole life. Inspiration is, it says, 'a divine influence or action on a person believed to qualify him or her to receive and communicate sacred revelation.' This is exactly what I felt Judith was doing that evening, being an inspirational conduit of something sacred that Life, through her, was presenting to me. And the revelation, well, that was the essence of simplicity really, for in those deeply quiet moments I spent by her side, I came to understand that the time had come to start sharing with others what I was experiencing with the cows.

At first, this took the form of posts made to a 'Being with Cows' Facebook page, and it soon became clear that even the process of trying to convert the experiences into words was itself going to be an act of meditation. To do justice to the depth of the discoveries made in the company of the cows, I wanted the words to be as accurate as possible, to somehow communicate the essence of what I was witnessing out in the meadows and woods. I wanted them to reach out and touch the reader, to give them a taste of what I was privileged to be experiencing first hand. This often meant becoming very quiet as the words were being typed, trusting that the quietness would then find its way into the post and that perhaps the reader could pick up on the stillness that held the words in place. The photos and especially the video clips that accompanied the words, however, often said more than even the most quietly and carefully scripted posts could ever do.

By the time 2017 wandered feebly in and an incredibly

mild winter gave way to spring, the Facebook page was beginning to attract some good interest. The response from certain followers was another source of inspiration and I was able to see that for some people, the mixture of meditation and moving stories about just what these so-called farm animals had to offer was in a way irresistible. Equine therapy is a well-established service that helps people reconnect with themselves through contact made with horses, and there is a raft of well-documented cases describing how many, including children considered to be on the autistic spectrum, have made profound breakthroughs in the presence of dolphins. Billions around the world can testify to the therapeutic effects of pet cats, dogs, rabbits, rats and so on. Why not then with cows?

When the number of followers on the page climbed up towards a thousand, there was some kind of satisfaction that the word was spreading, click-by-distant-click. One afternoon in April suddenly added another ingredient into the mix. I was sitting with some friends from the local area, parents who had started bringing their children to the farm to play with Gabi. As the kids made the most of a muddy puddle, splashing and smothering themselves from head to toe with clay, I began to share some of the experiences I'd had with the cows, who were grazing just below us. After some moments, all of the hairs began to stand up on my neck and I shivered several times as a quiet tingling ran up and down my spine. One of the fathers started to smile and as I babbled on in my broken French. I could see that he was genuinely moved by what was being shared. He didn't say anything simply because his eyes said it all for him – twinkling away with an inner glow that quickly brought my words to a close. We all sat quietly for some minutes, watching the cows going about their business. How funny, I thought, that the real sharing begins when the words dry up for a while. Blah, blah, blah, most of the time, round and round and really going nowhere.

Later that evening, as I told Diana about the experience with the mums and dads, I knew that the contact that was being made with others through social media was no longer enough and that I had to find a way to start getting people to the farm itself. There was something about actually being in the physical presence of the cows, the very same thing I'd witnessed earlier in the day with the parents, that was crucial to really driving home the message. I needed to start providing opportunities for people to come and sit with the cows, to get up close and look deeply into their eyes, to enter into their world of calm yet solid steadiness, for it was there, right by their shaggy sides, that the real contact could be made. Social media can of course provide so many wonderful platforms and opportunities for the sharing of stories, but there's nothing like getting up close and personal with the beauties themselves so that they, in their own quiet way, can tell you what all the fuss is really about.

# CHAPTER 6

# Reaching out

'There are those whose lives affect all others around them. Quietly touching one heart, who in turn, touches another. Reaching out to ends further than they would ever know.'

WILLIAM BRADFIELD

The first Being with Cows Retreats were advertised towards the end of spring 2017. Carried away on a wave of enthusiasm, I invested some of what little money I had on a Facebook campaign in an attempt to get the cows and

the farm into the public eye. The return on the investment was a lot more likes and follows on the FB page and several enquiries from people curious about the unusual mixture of cows and meditation, but not a single confirmed booking.

Some part of me wanted everything to fall perfectly into place and for guests to begin arriving by the busload. The briefest image of Cork flickering on and off in my mind's eye could sometimes lead to such a powerful desire to connect the cows with others that I often felt physically sick, unable to remain an impassive observer of such swirling emotions.

I then decided to look further afield and contacted several organisations involved in the promotion of ethical forms of livestock rearing, asking if they could feature an article about the cows.

Compassion in World Farming responded in a very supportive way and invited me to send photos of the cows for an article on their website and Facebook page. This was the first sign that the story behind the retreats did indeed hold an interest among a wider audience, other than just with the FB fanbase, and the posting of the article only reinforced the quiet confidence I carried, despite the emotional outbursts.

When it was published at the beginning of summer, the post stimulated the normal raft of likes and dislikes, smiley and angry faces and a small smattering of love-heart emojis. As I read the various comments, I noticed a certain irritability arising when I saw what I felt were glaring assumptions based upon emotion rather than clear fact.

# Reaching out

I was accused of killing cows in the name of profit, when not a single cow has ever left the farm for the abattoir. It felt as if the article was simply an opportunity for some to vent their angst and frustration at what they perceived to be just another example of mankind's exploitation of domesticated animals.

Arguments developed between people who had posted comments. Back and forth like a tennis ball, points of view were served and returned, at times with a savage ferocity.

My first instinct was to rage at some of the people posting online. I felt angry and deeply annoyed that, in my opinion [!], they hadn't even bothered to investigate what was happening on the farm thoroughly enough so as to be clear about what they were writing. There was a desire to want to crush such assumptions, but also to want to confront the person responsible for the comment.

It was in the midst of typing a reply to someone, a personal reaction to a comment about separating mothers from their calves, that, for a moment, the clouds parted and a clarity came shining through. Suddenly I could see that both sides of each argument were coming from the same root, the same source and origin – another perfectly timed mindful 'mind bomb' moment. It was clear that in reality, there is no separate self to create the mirage of one arguing against another. It is only when there is identification with the 'person' who is apparently making an argument, that the idea of such a sense of division, of me against him, her or them becomes possible. This persuasive something or other that convinces us of our apparent separateness and individuality is what is known as the ego. Thoughts are its materia prima. Mindfulness is seeing this exactly as it is, just watching those thoughts roll by. Self-help is learning to be mindful. Sounds easy, doesn't it?

As this sense of clear knowing deepened, it expanded to also include those people and posts expressing support for the article. The likes and smiley faces communicated no difference whatsoever from the dislikes and unhappy ones. Everything was just as it was without personal involvement.

When, after several minutes, the mental machinery cranked back into action again, I felt able to write clear responses to some of the posts, unhindered by desires to defend myself or my point of view. There was great motivation to write in accordance with this subtle inner feeling and not with the head or emotions and in so doing, I was honouring the essence of what I had experienced with the cows. If I succumbed to tit-for-tat games of push and shove online, I could no longer be truly said to be representing what Being with Cows stood for.

An example of the online exchange between people following the post developed like this:

Michelle Joanne: They still have tags in their ears and I'm worried that the tags make the animals into a commodity. With respect, what are your animals raised for?

Being with Cows Retreats: If you read somewhere above you will see that the Casta we raise here are a breeding herd to try to stabilise a critically endangered breed. They are native to the Central French Pyrenees, are incredibly intelligent and retain many of the instincts of their wild ancestors. It is a real privilege to be involved with them.

Michelle Joanne: So they won't be killed?

Being with Cows Retreats: I cannot speak for other breeders but we have never taken the life of any of our cows for meat.

Michelle Joanne: Now I'm happy. I've been vegetarian for thirty years and have now become vegan so I'm very sensitive. Love to you and glad that you truly love your beasts because there is so much about how farmers love their stock as they take them to slaughter.

Charlotte Dover: Ear tagging is mandatory under EU legislation. All livestock have to be tagged, whether kept as pets, or raised for breeding, meat or milk.

Jayne Rose: Being with Cows, that's lovely.


Even though I could feel a sense of disappointment when, with winter fast approaching, not a single guest had joined us on retreat, I remained buoyed by a quiet but clear confidence, which continued to tell me to be patient and that little by little, Life would draw guests to this beautifully rural corner of southern France.

All the attention that was centred on the retreats was pushed to one side, however, during the very last days of the year, for into our life came the gurgling little bundle named Elie. A brother for Gabi! Pure and utter delight. Thrilled, besotted and immediately thinking of Cork. Diana was convinced that she had been carrying a girl, yet out he popped in all his wrinkled splendour. Gabi and myself nicknamed him The Mole. We couldn't help it, what with the shape of his tiny little face and especially the way he wriggled his shiny nose. Gabi, making a masterful effort to keep any sense of jealousy at bay, seemed delighted.

When I first carried him to the cows, the Galloways then the Casta, it was with a deeply powerful sense of family that I entered their meadows. If hearts can truly sing, then mine was fairly filling the sky with song as I introduced him to his captivated audience. They sniffed and snorted, tried many times to lick his little face and genuinely seemed thrilled to be making his acquaintance. The youngsters in both herds were particularly eager to meet him, tiptoeing forward yet ready to reverse at the slightest hint of trouble.

Valentine, as always, the boldest and least suspicious of the lot, nudged her way through the crowd to stand by our side. Holding Elie in my arms, I shifted round to her front end, so that she could get a proper view of him and then, without any qualms whatsoever, placed him gently on her back. I hadn't planned to do anything of the kind but seeing his tiny little fingers grabbing hold of her winter fur put the smile of all smiles on my grateful face.

Another advertising campaign through the winter and early spring of 2018 had generated much greater interest, yet again without leading to actual reservations being made.

This all changed when I received an enquiry for the retreat advertised for the end of April. The first booking was swiftly followed by another and even though it wasn't as if the floodgates had opened, at least it was a start.

# CHAPTER 7

# Retreats

'Meditation could be said to be the Art of Simplicity:
simply sitting, simply breathing and simply being.'

DILGO KHYENTSE RINPOCHE

The very first retreat unfolded in its own organic way
and proved to be something of a microcosm of all that I
had experienced so far with the cows. There was a rough
structure to it – meditational walks in the mornings and
mindful sessions with the cows in the afternoon – but
apart from that I had no wish to try to fill every minute
with organised activity. It was the cows themselves who
had impressed on me so deeply this alignment with
rhythms borne not of the mind but some deeper undercurrent, a trust that the quietness brings all into its own
order.

When it had become clear that I wanted to begin
inviting guests to the farm on retreat, the brainstorming
of ideas regarding the structure and form they might take
didn't really get off the ground. It wasn't needed – the
thinking about things. That time would be spent with

the cows was obvious yet I knew that something else could complement the sessions with them, something a little more active that had to involve the landscape that I had fallen in love with. The feeling of wanting to share everything I felt grateful for had become a powerful guiding force since the acceptance of Cork's death, and it was this that brought the understanding that the essential ingredient had to be simplicity. The foundation of whatever might unroll on retreat had to be free of techniques, teachings and anything that desired to produce any kind of result, whether it was mindfully beneficial or not. This much was absolutely clear. The *being* part of Being with Cows said it all. The sharing had to express all that I loved about the cows and the beautiful land round about in the simplest way possible and one of the simplest things I knew was walking.

It had long been something very important to me, a vital activity that was as natural as breathing in and out, and the cows themselves spent at the very least half of their days ambling around wherever they happened to be. Putting feet on the earth, particularly in a natural environment, usually provided an incredibly levelling experience, a quite literal grounding of all that was surplus to requirements at any given time.

The walks therefore were made in silence, a chance to be together with the landscape, each other and whatever arose in a way that wasn't dominated by talk. This temporary suspension of chit-chat was of course also inspired by the cows. In all the countless hours that I'd spent with them, I'd realised that their need to vocalise things was absolutely minimal. Hunger, giving birth or excitement at moving to fresh grazing might lead to their calls echoing around the valleys, but other than that, their communication was non-verbal and they passed their days in silence. It seemed natural then that the retreats would end up reflecting this, becoming more of an extension of what was already present on the farm rather than something new imposed on it.

Some mornings were spent on the tracks that crisscrossed the farm while others took us out into the surrounding valleys and hills. What a time to be out and about, in the full flush of spring and all that it could bring. Both of the guests were already committed nature-lovers and at times it brought a genuine sense of joy to be strolling our way up and down the hills together, untroubled by comment or conversation.

At times we would stop and sit a while. Some places that I'd discovered in the years since we'd arrived on the farm seemed to naturally lend themselves to meditation, to a sitting in quietness and something else as well. They were places where I'd experienced a deeply touching calmness, a warmth and unlooked-for feeling of safety that was a kind of homecoming. I've heard them called sit-spots by some, places where stillness becomes an immediate reality rather than something to wish for or desire. They are supportive little niches woven seamlessly into the landscape and are often not obvious at first sight.

Over and over I had witnessed the cows returning to the same patch of meadow or part of a woodland glade that, on the surface at least, looked no different from everything else around. Watching them purposely moving to these favoured spots had impressed me deeply. It was fascinating to observe that they were aware of things that mostly seem to have been buried beneath endless layers of restlessness and thinking.

On the second day of the retreat, the walk took us up to the highest point in the area – a set of oak-covered hills and green, meadow-softened valleys. As we wound our way up the hunters' track to the top, I indicated to the guests that we could stop for some moments and sit down. From where we sat, the views out and across towards the Pyrenees further south were simply magnificent. In equal measure, they inspired both an urge to talk and express wonder at such natural beauty *and* the necessity of keeping the mouth firmly closed in quiet appreciation of their majesty. The invitation was to let them do all the talking, and the initial idea of spending just a few minutes gave way to an hour or more of quiet gazing. Rain-laden clouds that we could almost reach out and touch, miles of sparkling greenery too perfect to name and an undeniably refreshing smell of spring in the air had us naturally stilled into silence.

When we arrived back at the farm a while later and the walk had officially finished, I noticed that none of us were so keen to break the silence with words. Walking and talking is fine in itself, yet over the course of the last few hours, we had tapped into something that removed the need to say anything at all.

The weather was a typically April assortment of sunshine and short sharp showers, a rainbow-making mixture that signalled the onset of spring in her prime. At times, I knew that the guests were connecting with the landscape and the cows in ways that made my heart sing. The early orchids were beginning to claim the meadows as their own, purple ranks of beauty pushing up above the turf, and the sound of croaking frogs filled the valley from one end to the other.

When it came to the first afternoon session with the cows, I could barely contain my excitement. This was it, the moment I'd been waiting for since the idea for the retreats first appeared. It was to be with the Casta, for by then both they and the Galloways had young bulls in attendance and each breed was separated from the other.

Before entering the patch of open woodland where they were, I spent several minutes talking about their history, their undeserved reputation for stubbornness, but also of the need to stay alert and aware of what was going on around us. Being mindful definitely doesn't mean drifting off into some dreamy haze, and I reminded the guests that although the cows were docile and calm, they were, at the end of the day, large, powerful animals that required our utmost respect and regard. I couldn't predict what might happen, how the cows would react or respond to suddenly having a small group of relative strangers in their midst. It was as much an unknown for me as it was for anyone else and perhaps because of this I took the time to reassure both guests that I would be constantly monitoring the atmosphere in the group and ready to step in if I saw any sign of nervousness or unusual behaviour in the cows. I also invited them to let me know if any difficulties arose or if they felt that the cows had come in too close for comfort.

Instinctively, I trusted that all would be well. I couldn't feel anything else but confidence in the picture that Life was painting for us. The first few moments with the Casta were characterised by their complete and utter lack of interest in us. They continued to graze and nibble on the newly opened oak leaves with barely a glance in our direction. Due to my refusal to stage-manage anything at all with regard to the cows, the place where we had found them didn't naturally lend itself to sitting quietly in their presence. The mixture of scrubby undergrowth and youngish oak made it easy for the Casta to disappear in the blink of an eye and it wasn't until we followed them up onto the more open areas at the top of the hill that we could really see them in all their glory.

They continued to remain aloof, going about their business seemingly unaffected by our presence. Typical Casta . . . everything kept within! Let nothing out, at all costs. Burn it all, deep down in the bottom of the basement.

After an hour or so we left them to it and, on the way to see the Galloways, I asked the guests what they had experienced during their first close-up contact with the Casta. It was no surprise to hear that at first, particularly in the scrubby woodland where open space was at a premium, both of the guests had felt a little unnerved. They pretty much said the same thing – that the terrain, in combination with the genuinely powerful presence of the impressively horned Casta, had led them to feel squeezed, somehow, restricted and even unsettled. The lack of surprise I experienced at what was shared was simply because their words echoed my own during my first few weeks with the Casta. I too had been somehow disturbed, afraid even at times and left wondering on occasion what the hell these things were about? Great shiny mirrors, that's what, beautiful breathing reflectors of all that comes to their door.

Both guests confirmed, however, that once we moved into the wooded meadow higher up, the open space allowed them to relax, to breathe easy and enjoy peering in through the window that the opportunity presented. At a safe and respectful distance, they could finally get a taste of all that I'd been sharing since their arrival a couple of days earlier. They did indeed feel touched by the Casta and equally so by the beauty of the landscape around us. It was not something that was easy to define, one of them said, being such an unusual mixture of mindfulness in the midst of cows.

What it had already revealed, very quickly and quite obviously for one of them, was an undercurrent of rest-lessness, a background kind of edgy disquiet that she had experienced during most of the session. She hadn't even known quite how fidgety she was until she got to sit with the herd.

If the Casta had displayed their natural form of shyness,

the Galloways were all interest and curiosity. When we entered their streamside meadow, they came quietly over to see what we were up to. Valentine, as normal, led the way. She planted herself firmly in front of me, flicking her head gently from side to side, telling me to get on with it, the daily scratch and pat on her back. It made such a happy scene when she allowed the guests to join in for a moment or two, particularly after the start they'd had with the Casta.

When the idea for the retreats had come along, physical contact with the cows wasn't seen as a priority. Many other farms and sanctuaries around the world had begun to offer cow-hugging experiences, where guests could pay to get really close and cosy, quite literally embracing whatever the cow in question had to offer. If that happened during a retreat at our place, all well and good, yet at no time whatsoever had it ever been envisaged as something that would be overtly offered. 'Whatever will be, will be' was the mantra.

Now that Valentine was there among us, I was genuinely happy, and what pleased me most was that the encounter had happened without coercion on anyone's part. It had all unfolded quite naturally, without planning or even desire to make it so; *que sera sera*.

Sitting still with the cows allowed us the chance to immerse ourselves not only in their world, but the world around us too. This was the pinnacle for me – that the cows and their unhurried ways were capable of bringing us into such quietness that suddenly it seemed as if the doors to nature's very own treasury had been flung wide open. Birds became less timid, for we posed them no threat, and the quality of their songs soared in that space vacated by thought and thinking.

It was becoming ever more clear, particularly as I could now observe the interactions of the guests with the cows, that the Galloways and Casta could, among many things, act as some sort of brake, slowing down the pace of our often frantically hurried lives. They invited us to breathe easy, to take the foot off the pedal and drop down into a quiet watching of our thoughts. On the last day, one of the guests shared again that she hadn't realised just how very speedy her daily life was, restlessness ruling the roost, until she stopped spinning from one thing to another. That the cows were able to be such solid full stops at the end of so many rambling sentences was a source of much joy and even relief, especially as the retreat drew to a close.

I say relief without any hesitation, because sometime on the third or fourth day, I became aware of a nagging anxiety that had me wondering if the guests were benefitting in any way from their stay on the farm. It was clear for me that the mixture of activities and the gentle invitation to watch the thoughts coming and going was something that could lead one into a deeply meditative state and experience of quietness. However, I began to speculate on the fact that there may have appeared to be nothing on offer for people who had paid good money and come in search of something tangible, a tool or two, perhaps, with which to make a noticeable difference to their lives. No one was trying to teach anybody anything. There were no guided meditations, no mention of breath-control techniques or invitations to follow any particular method or discipline.

There was at times a nervousness in the way I went about things. It seemed connected to the uncertainty I had in inviting the guests to simply be quiet. A nagging voice would suddenly pipe up, crowing from the treetops that they were bored, that they needed more than just sitting in a field full of cows and that they would benefit by being given a little more in the way of direction. The truth is I didn't feel capable of guiding anyone anywhere. How could I justifiably do anything of the kind when I still didn't know who I was? And this, after all, was the whole point about the retreats; they had emerged out of the ashes of a deeply painful event, grabbed me by the scruff of the neck and pulled me along for the ride. What was downloaded in the cows' company, several months before, never for a single moment mentioned anything to do with anyone playing the role of a teacher or guide. It just wasn't about that.

All of this concern, however, while not fading away completely, did loosen its often vice-like grip on the last afternoon of the retreat. Gazing softly at the cows, I suddenly realised that I too was on retreat, as much of a guest as those who had paid to be there and that, inevitably, the extended periods of silence in which we sat or walked would bring things up in me too. Once this had been acknowledged, that quiet confidence came surging back in, a resolute, inner conviction that the retreats were fine as they were. The uncertainty was just for letting go of another cloud that covered the sun, but one that I now knew would sail on its way when I remembered the light up above it.

# CHAPTER 8

# Momentum

'Your hardest times often lead to the greatest moments
of your life. Keep going. Tough situations build strong
people in the end.'

ROY BENNETT

The next two guests joined the retreat in June. One of them,
Bonnie, worked for the Sustainable Food Trust in the UK.
According to their website, the SFT's mission statement is:

'We work to accelerate the transition to more sustainable food and farming systems that nourish the health
of both people and planet. To achieve this, we work
catalytically and collaboratively, with an emphasis on
communication, education and thought leadership.'

Well, the cows we share the land with aren't being raised
for food and I can't even claim that we qualify as typical
members of the farming community, yet I was happy to
have an employee of such an influential organisation
joining us.

I was even more delighted when Bonnie invited me to write an article for the SFT's newsletter. It seemed another step on from the article with Compassion in World Farming, for which I'd been able to contribute some beautiful photos, but not any description of the retreats or the story behind them. When such opportunities began to occur, often without any effort on my part, I began to feel so clearly that it was Life itself who wished the farm to gain recognition from a wider audience. There was no pleasure personally speaking, that 'my' writing was gaining attention, that I would see my name in print and so on, for in reality, I couldn't claim to really have done anything at all. All I could feel was Life doing what it needed to do, using the farm, the cows and even Corky's death as a way to bring more of its flock back into the fold.

Here is the article as it appeared in the newsletter:

Being with Cows

It was in the middle of October 2015, on a warm and sunny autumnal afternoon, when I got the news. My younger brother had committed suicide. He was supposed to be visiting us on the farm three days later, yet it just wasn't meant to be.

Five weeks later, on returning from the family home in Worcestershire, I went straight to the wooded hillside where our cows, the Galloways and Castas, had been in our absence.

Perhaps it was the events of the preceding weeks that stirred the emotions, who knows, yet on calling them, hearing them respond and eventually seeing their heads poking out of the woodland edge, tears came to the eyes and for a moment, all the grief just slipped away.

Over the coming weeks, as autumn rolled into winter and the twice-daily round of feeding the cows began, I found myself becoming ever more grateful just to be in the presence of the six heifers we had at the time.

The Galloways, short, stocky and snug in their winter coats. The Castas, sleek, agile and already in possession of a fine set of black-tipped horns. Without a tractor and set of forks to lift the round bales of our own hay into the feeder, the contact with them during feeding time was always [and continues to be] up close and intimate.

The passing of my brother seemed to have effected a change in the way things were seen and it appeared, with the cows in particular, that their characters, their habits and their funny little ways were suddenly visible in a way not previously imagined.

There was already an unshakable commitment to raising them in as natural a way as possible. When the farm was bought, it had been certified organic for 25 years.

There was a history of respect, of pesticide-free, compassion-based farming already in the soil and I'm sure that as we began to put down roots of our own, they simply connected with something wholesome and alive that was already here.

As the months went on, I found myself spending as much time with the cows as possible, whether it was feeding them, fixing fences around them or freeing-up more grazing by clearing away stands of bramble and thick scrub.

At the time, I felt something akin to some kind of magnetism, pulling me ever onwards in their direction and it came to me one day that the grieving for my brother stopped whenever I was in their company. They were helping me heal without any effort at all, simply by being with them.

Within six months, I felt little or no pain in relation to the loss. There was only acceptance, and the hole in the stomach that had sometimes felt like a bottomless pit was filled with the warmth of gratitude – for having known my brother and for just how effortlessly the cows had helped me to heal.

Now, at the time of writing, the cows have led us deeper and deeper into their ways. There are currently seven Galloways and ten Castas. The two breeds are separated and each has a fine young bull to keep the heifers and cows company.

The Galloway heifers have become wonderful mothers and only last week we saw the birth of our first beautiful little Casta calf. This is a particularly joyous occasion, as the Casta breed remains critically endangered.

This once iconic and most populous breed of the central French Pyrenees is down to a population of around 350 breeding cows.

Our commitment to the most natural form of livestock farming has only intensified and it is without doubt a result of knowing each calf, heifer, cow and bull as a living, breathing being worthy of our utmost respect, attention and care.

Reading the reissued edition of Rosamund Young's gem of a book *The Secret Life of Cows* has only served to reinforce the sense that everything that is happening here is the naturally right way to go about the rearing of livestock. What a wonderful way to receive such a confirmation!

It is then almost with a sense of reverence that I go to the cows each morning, to see how they are doing and perhaps to listen to what they can tell me of the day to come.

It is they who reflect back the wisdom of natural care, their shining coats and eyes that speak of a diet of grasses and herbs, of abundant wildflowers and acorns in autumn. I've even seen the Castas eating mushrooms when the season is on us.

Both herds overwinter outside, in meadows and woodland that are sacrificed for the purpose. The hay they are fed is sourced as locally as possible, always comes from organic, flower-rich meadows and is the only supplementary feed they get during the year.

They are antibiotic, disease-free cattle, living in as close a way as we can possibly manage to the life that their wild ancestors may have lived before domestication arrived. It is their innate intelligence that informs me of what is best for them. In an atmosphere of mutual trust, where learning to listen to the language they speak is of the utmost importance, they themselves will indicate all that is needed to be done.

Being sensitive to this has granted access to what feels like the inner workings of the herd and from this position there comes ever more enthusiasm to provide the very best conditions possible for their health and wellbeing. It is a way of saying thank you to them for the way in which they enrich our lives.

Recently, they have begun to be treated homeopathically. For example, two of the Galloway calves had developed quite severe warts on their heads and necks. A single treatment of ten granules of Thuja 10c for each calf, in combination with a vigorous dosing and rubbing of each wart with organic cider vinegar, had them both wart-free within a week. The cider vinegar has also proved to be incredibly successful in treating external maladies such as ringworm.

In emergency situations, such as a potentially fatal tick infestation in spring or a damper than usual autumn, the vet will be called and their advice taken, if it means the saving of a life. Yet less and less is this course of action necessary.

Farming in a way that specifically encourages vibrantly healthy ecosystems in the form of diversity-rich meadows, woodland and streams really does seem to automatically reduce the cows' susceptibility to disease and illness.

As much as it is a farm, we like to see the land we look after as a sanctuary for all forms of wildlife. Management work involving brush-cutters and chainsaws only happens in winter when amphibians, birds, insects and reptiles are less active. Large stands of blackthorn, bramble, hawthorn and gorse are left untouched to provide as much habitat as possible for wild boar, roe deer, fox, pine marten, a host of nesting birds and the elusive genet.

It may seem too simplistic, too child-like and naïve in an age of almost forensically intense analysis, but a happy land really does mean happy cows and happy cows can mean happy farmers who may want to share something about the joys of their happy discovery.

This spring, we welcomed our first guests to the farm, to participate in a retreat, simply entitled 'Being with Cows'. The retreats, which are held once a month from April through to October, are another way of saying thank you to the cows, to the land and to the wildlife that so enrich our lives here on the farm.

After the death of my brother, the cows quite simply helped me to heal and I began to wonder if they could touch others in the same way. It was out of this reflection that the idea for the retreats came and slowly took hold. I simply wanted to share the rich seam of gold I felt I had discovered. Perhaps they could soothe a troubled mind and stop, if but for a moment, the spinning of an increasingly frantic world?

By now, this part of southern France was settling into summer and the retreat unfolded under mostly clear blue skies. All the forests were by now in full leaf and alive with the frantic activity of nesting birds. The native ranks had been swelled by the seasonal influx of migrators and the odd flash of turquoise or crimson feathers brought a sense of the exotic to the landscape. The bee-eaters in particular, glinting all green and royal gold in the sunshine, were a delight to behold. This was the time of the solstice, and the long mellow evenings were often spent wild-life-watching in the local area. Mostly we would go to a place but a stone's throw from the farm, where an old track wound its way around the feet of several shallow valleys. It was here, away from any roads or buildings of any kind, that we could watch the red and roe deer come out to play, the fauns emerging from the woodland edge to dance in the dappled light.

During such moments, I felt at times almost pressed into the earth under the weight of gratitude. Along with the cows and my family, this is where my heart lay and to be sharing it with others left me feeling deeply grateful, thankful that Cork's passing had somehow led to moments such as these.

The cows, by now, were getting more used to the presence of visitors and were less timid when we went and sat among them. Both the Casta and the Galloways had expanded their ranks. All the Galloways, thanks to the presence of a fine young bull we had named Leith, had calved and the first precious and beautiful little Casta had made her way into the world shortly before, much to the delight not only of her proud mama but the rest of the herd, too.

Valentine and her son Nairn were the most approachable of all. I had developed such a bond of trust with her that when Nairn was born (our very first calf on the entire farm) and I found him curled up on the forest floor beside a big oak, she left him with me and went off to graze, bringing tears to my grateful eyes. Now, she would allow the guests to come to her side, to stroke her for a while, absorbing some sense of her calm through their fingertips.

While the retreats were never advertised as being of the cow-cuddling kind, some of which were beginning to receive a lot of attention in the media, I was happy that on occasion, guests could make physical contact with them. The decision always rested with the cows them-selves; they were never tied up or encouraged with snacks of one kind or another in order to satisfy a desire to stroke them. It couldn't be like that. If they wanted contact of this kind, then that was entirely up to them. Never for a moment did I wish to impose anything upon them that they wouldn't have done in the natural course of things. In light of this, when they did amble over to be touched, it felt as if a cleaner, purer contact was being made. I had no intent of ever trying to influence what might happen on retreat, not with the guests nor the cows neither. What I *did* have to do, and was shown very clearly during this retreat, was to get my own thoughts and head-fuzz right out of the way; doing so would mean that whatever happened was aligned with the unthinking spirit in which I felt the cows continually lived.

I trusted this process implicitly, not only in relation to the retreats and the cows but in all aspects of my life. Nothing was pressed or forced. If I tried to do so, it invariably came splatting back straight in my face. This process of letting go was total and once it got hold of you there was no escape. When this was accepted and commitment made to keeping it in mind, quite wonderful things could happen.

It was only a week after the June retreat had finished and our family life had returned to its own version of normality that I received a very unexpected phone call. I was playing with Gabi on the lawn, pretending to pull tractors and Lego aeroplanes from his ears, when Diana came out and said someone wanted to speak to me about the cows. As I took the phone from her, I was half expecting it to be the vet or one of the neighbours telling me that the cows had gone walkabout, again. So much for expectations!

The ensuing conversation went something like this:

'Hello.'

'Hi. Can I speak to Dave Mountjoy?'

'Yeah, speaking.'

'Hi, Dave. My name's Chris Holmes and I work for a company called Oxford Scientific Films. We've been commissioned by the BBC to make a documentary series about farm animals. It's got the working title of *The Secret Life of Farm Animals* and your farm in France has come to our attention. We've heard you've got some unusual stuff going on with your cows and we were wondering if you might be interested in us coming down to film for a few days during your next retreat. I believe it's one that includes yoga. Is that right?

'Yeah, that's right, it does. I think it starts around 27 July but I'll have to check that for you. And yeah, of course, please come. I'm a bit amazed really, I mean, that you've got in touch, that you're actually interested in our little place. No, it's great, really great. I'm well up for it. In fact, I'm in shock really, a bit shocked, yeah. Christ, the BBC.'

Could it actually be, the BBC really en route to our own dust-covered little doorstep? Was the light that began as a glint in Judith's eye really becoming such a powerful beam, enough to flash its compassionate code out into the wider world? Had Cork's passing, in some way, really led to this?

Oh yes, my great fool of a brother . . . oh yes.

## CHAPTER 9

# The BBC

Ego says, 'Once everything falls into place, I'll feel peace.'
Spirit says, 'Find your peace, and then everything will fall into place.'

MARIANNE WILLIAMSON

In between the first phone call with Chris and the beginning of the retreat three weeks later, I felt myself to be the privileged recipient of an indefinable gift. Daily life continued as normal and preparations for the five days of yoga and cow-bathing were well in hand, but something so subtle as to be barely detectable seemed to have set up camp in my mind. It quickly removed the habitual round of thoughts and thinking and replaced them with something soft yet deeply self-assured. It was as if the imminent arrival of the film crew and the continued sense of surprise that they were actually coming at all propelled me into a state of such relaxation that I wandered around on automatic pilot. I hardly slept but felt no tiredness at all. Everything felt so effortless that at times I waited for the bubble to burst but it didn't, it just kept on expanding, drawing all inside its walls.

Most of all, though, those days leading up to the beginning of the retreat were punctuated by the distinct feeling of being *moved*. The whole thing felt like a set-up; something greater than anything I could possibly imagine was simply pushing me wherever I needed to go. When I brought attention to this feeling, it seemed achingly obvious that the *something* had also organised and arranged the forthcoming visit of the folk from Oxford Scientific Films. I was well and truly caught in a most wonderfully blissful web, supported in all ways by so many unseen strands upon which I lay in total confidence. In quiet moments, usually with the cows, I understood that it is always like this but that the incessant chatter upstairs in the head does a perfect job of blocking out all comprehension. Shakespeare's oft-quoted 'All the world's a stage' felt more accurate than ever, the wisest appraisal of what we call our waking daily life – nothing more than our very own private film-set upon which we as actors tread the boards.

In the last few days before the retreat began, I spent as much time as possible with the cows. The deepening of the sensitivity I was experiencing in myself was reflected in the increasingly still and mindful exchanges I had with them. I was convinced they could feel the depths into which I'd unknowingly plunged, especially the Casta. When I moved among them, they would remain stock still, in what appeared to be complete acceptance of my presence. Up until then, some of them had still backed away when I walked through the herd, their natural timidity setting feet in backward motion whenever I came too close. With Judith, this admittance into what I felt to be the Castas' inner sanctum led to the most tender of exchanges. Resting our foreheads against each other, we locked into some quite wonderful moments – of what I cannot say. If I try to describe it, attempt to force the formless into squiggles on a page, it just isn't going to work, all square pegs and round holes. All I can honestly say is that a melting took place and quietly leave it at that.

When the retreat began on the last Friday in July, we were a group of seven altogether. It was the first time that yoga had been offered to guests and I was curious to see how the practising of postures would play out in the presence of the Galloways. They had been moved to the meadows high up on a valley side where the yoga sessions would take place each morning. The wooden platform that would host the classes looked out across miles of forest and hilltops to the majestic peaks of the Pyrenees and, during the introductory tour of the farm, I could already see that the combination of the landscape and the untroubled way in which the Galloways greeted the guests was laying the foundation for the wonderful days to come.

The film team arrived on the Saturday afternoon for a meeting with myself and the guests, to ensure all parties were in accord and happy with the format for the filming. Once we were all in agreement, the filming proper began early on the Sunday morning, with a yoga session high up on the meadow facing the Pyrenees.

In preparation for the team's arrival, I'd been feeding the Galloways for several days with some hay, scattered around the foot of the wooden platform. It felt a bit like cheating, trying to ensure that the guests could be filmed stretching and flexing while surrounded by the on-looking cows, but the moment I saw the interaction of the guests and Galloways as Janina, the yoga teacher, took them through their first session, any lingering sense of artificiality just slipped away.

Knowing the cows as I did, the whole scene was pure and joyous theatre. From Leith the powerful bull right down to Valentine's young calf Nairn, the whole herd stood and watched the group go through their routines. I wouldn't dare to speculate on what the cows might have been experiencing during those heady moments, but if my own inner feelings were any kind of barometer for the general atmosphere, then peace reigned supreme. There was a tangible sense of magic in the air, nothing exaggerated or entertaining but downright calm and quiet and naturally so.

When Janina began to sing and play the harmonium towards the end of the class, it seemed that the whole valley stopped to listen. Most of the Galloways had by then already sauntered away to graze but July, heavily pregnant and ready to calve, not only stayed behind but rested her head on the smooth boards of the platform, entranced it seemed by the soothing quality of the sounds.

Later in the day, during the lunch break, I continued working with the film team. I was invited by the cameraman to walk in among the Galloways, who had by then retired to a shady spot several hundred yards from the wooden platform.

He asked me to walk slowly into the midst of the group and do whatever came naturally. Something wasn't quite right for him during the first two takes, yet with the third, everything clicked quite perfectly into place.

As I made my way into the middle of the small herd, Nairn seemed to make space for me between him and his mama, so I knelt down and started to stroke her head and neck. As the camera continued to roll, the thinking and thoughts began to slow down, until there came a point when I simply wasn't aware of any mental activity at all. There was nothing but warmth, such warmth and peace and solitude. No cows existed to be stroked, no trees to cast shade nor even sun to shine down on it all. There was simply IT, the something that is everything, which denies all attempt at division. It's not to say that, visually speaking, nothing was visible anymore, but that the capacity to separate things into individual pieces had simply evaporated.

At the peak of this deeply meditative state, Valentine, beautiful shining Valentine, went to sleep in my arms. Resting her great shaggy head in my lap, it felt as if she was doing her own version of purring like a cat! As her breathing slowed down, so mine did too. How could so many kilos of furry head and neck feel like no more than a feather in my hands? It was incredibly hot, one of those sweltering days without even a hint of breeze to shift the solid air, and normally speaking I would have long since run for shelter in the forest's shade. However, with the temporary suspension of all thought, there was no one at home to feel bothered by the heat, and all was refreshingly cool. Flies buzzed, tails constantly swished and sweat trickled and dripped from my face, splashing at times onto Valentine's glistening nose, but all was so perfectly well.

I don't know how long we stayed like that, Valentine and me. It could have been forever as far as I was concerned. It was only when the cameraman shouted out that he'd 'Got it!' that the spell was broken. I could see from his face that he was very happy with what he'd captured on film, and even though I tried in some way to respond, the words just wouldn't come. Actually, I didn't want to talk at all. To speak was an effort in itself but more than that, I didn't want words to pierce that deep and devastating stillness. Devastating because for a while it had blown or washed everything clean away. To the ego, this is devastation.

The feeling of union with her was so complete that even though the experience is retold here in words, no words can ever do justice to such a meeting.

There are many reports of life-changing encounters with holy people, with saints and sages from down the ages. Why not with animals too? Of course, there are a billion and more pet owners around the world who can testify to the love and care they are given by the animals they share their homes with. Cats and dogs and rabbits, hamsters, rats and snakes . . . the list goes on and on. Why not too with cows? Great lovable, sweet-smelling inky-eyed cows.

The rest of the retreat passed by in an air of unremitting joy. The group seemed utterly together, a single unit of apparently different parts, each one charged with their own version of self-discovery. We walked in such silence, sat for hour upon hour with the Casta and Galloways, and like so many little sponges, soaked up all that the landscape had to offer.

All the anxieties I had experienced the previous year in relation to the retreats – whether the guests would benefit from what was on offer – failed to ripple what felt like a perfectly smooth surface. My whole experience was one of sitting in the very backseat, hands off the wheel, being driven wherever Life deemed necessary. I try to avoid as much as possible such clichés as *going with the flow*, yet it really did feel just like that.

And there were such moments of pure comedy too. At breakfast one morning, one of the guests recounted his experiences very early that morning with one of the Galloways in the forest. He had decided to sling his hammock somewhere in the trees, wanting to immerse himself deeply in the natural environment, to be hooted at by owls in the night and woken by songbirds at sunrise. He was a naturally gifted storyteller and he told his eager audience that in the murky half-light of dawn, he had sensed something moving slowly around his hammock. It had been strung quite high up off the ground to avoid any untoward contact with the wild boar that crossed the woodland each night, so he didn't feel unduly concerned, but when Isi, the most inquisitive of all the cows on the farm, suddenly popped her head inside, bringing it to within several centimetres of his own, he said that he sat bolt upright, not quite knowing whether to laugh or cry out.

Happily, calmness prevailed. Isi moved away to graze and Felix was left with memories of his close encounter and an unusual story to tell.

During the final session of the retreat, there came what could be called the icing on the cake. Whenever I'd sat with local kids, families or paying guests in the company of the cows, I'd been under the impression that it was us who had come to see them, to watch them going about their numerous little ways. Now, suddenly, the tables were quite wonderfully turned, for in sitting there that late afternoon, I received a very different understanding of what was happening when we sat in their presence; after all the hullabaloo about sitting down to observe them, it dawned on me that we were not in fact coming to see, but rather to be *seen*. Click. The lights came on again; another unveiling of yet another layer of cow-inspired insight. While sitting watching them go quietly about their business, we were in fact granting the cows unlimited access to all that we were bringing to the table – emotions, hang-ups, ideas and the background hum of thoughts whirring round and round. It felt so achingly obvious at the time that I laughed, chuckling to myself in delight at such a discovery. The cows, for me, sit in an almost permanent state of deeply embedded mindfulness. Therefore, it seemed quite logical that anything or anyone brought into their presence would be touched by the sheer force of such stillness, and the more quiet the mind could become, the greater the capacity for accessing this absolute treasure-trove of unlooked-for gold, of which they were the undisputed keepers. Being with them could become a constant round of spring cleaning, circular at first then spiralling down into the deepest roots of our being.

For a while there came a tidal surge of memories, images of the Casta or Galloways looking me up and down in such quizzical ways. I remembered that I always felt they were scanning me on such occasions, the laser-like force of their gaze penetrating to my very core. The Casta in particular regularly begin the first meeting of the day with a head-jiggling performance, scything the air with their horns in great rounded sweeps. It can look incredibly aggressive to the uninitiated, yet sitting there that afternoon it was clear that this was simply their way of reading what it was one was bringing to them. Their love of purity runs so deeply in their veins that they just can't tolerate giddy behaviour, and this instinctive assessment that is activated at each new contact ensures that they are able to act in ways that for them are the most appropriate for their safety and wellbeing. But . . . when they let you in and trust you, well, it's anchors at the ready, because step by steady step, they are going to pull you deeper and deeper into their world, down into realms of commitment and real responsibility. What they demand is total honesty, as they themselves live. Who do you think you are, they ask and then, who are you beyond thought? 'Take care' for them is a serious business and ultimately translates into that question of 'who am I?'

When the session came to its natural conclusion, and

with it, the heightened sense of awareness, I felt it had been the perfect way to bring to a close what had been a most perfect retreat. The presence of the film crew had added an extra ingredient to the time we spent together and it seemed that Life responded by bringing the very best out of all concerned – the group, the film crew themselves, and most of all, the cows. I'd never seen them so calm, so approachable and so very available as they were during those days. They rose to the occasion like seasoned old professionals, seizing the day in ways I could never have imagined, and as I fell asleep that night, I suddenly thought of Cork, of the gift his passing had become and how, given time and quiet determination, even the most unbearable grief can give way to peace and a trust in Life's undoubted compassion.

# CHAPTER 10

# *Cowfulness* – the art of farming mindfully

'Sit with animals quietly and they will show you their hearts. Sit with them kindly and they will help you locate yours.'

RAMBLINGS OF THE CLAURY

The next morning, after the last guests had departed, I sought out both groups of cows to say thank you. Thank you for the honesty they bring to our lives, for the reminder of calm and quietness, but most of all for simply being who they are, unfettered by need of attention or applause. It is this, I felt, that makes their presence in the world a rarely acknowledged gift to mankind. Gandhi himself bestowed upon them a most beautiful description, calling them 'poems of compassion', to be revered, cherished and valued for both their natural peacefulness and their ability to evoke the deeply maternal instincts of nurturing, caring and self-sacrifice in those who come into close, intimate contact with them.

I knew that whatever had been captured on film would somehow communicate the essence of these virtues, raising awareness of what are, generally speaking, mostly hidden qualities, and placing not only the cows I was blessed to be with, but perhaps all farm animals, in a different light.

In the days and weeks that followed the retreat, I wallowed in the luxury of having very few thoughts to pester me. Everyday life continued as normal – the daily round of looking after the cows and being bombarded by the demands of two lively and organically powered young boys – but the quietness that had welled up during the days of filming continued to trickle away in the background. Being with the cows really did mean *being*. The whole relationship with them morphed once again, shedding its skin to reveal an even smoother and shinier layer below. It wasn't that they became more physically available, standing in line to be stroked or anything of the kind, but there was an obvious deepening of trust. The Casta became even less guarded and had cast off more layers of the reserve and stubbornness for which they were traditionally famous. The Galloways just got even more placid, solid furry bundles of everything-is-ok.

This sense of increased togetherness and the effect it was having on my ability to practise mindfulness in all aspects of my life found a perfect description in a phrase that came bubbling up a month after the film crew's visit. Heavy August thunderstorms, spectacularly charged after weeks of intense heat, had cleared the sultry air and ushered in very welcome days of fresher temperatures. The parched landscape seemed to offer up an almost audible sigh of relief and the cows benefited from a flush of fresh grass that suddenly shot up out of nowhere.

I had just moved the Casta from a patch of woodland into one of the streamside meadows to graze. After several minutes of watching them – the gentle rising and falling of their chests, the swish of each tail flicking away the ever-present flies – I walked over to Judith to give her a scratch. Resting my face upon her broad back, I gazed out over the rest of the herd. All was calm and into the calmness came *cowfulness*. It just walked right in unannounced. 'Cowfulness,' I said out loud and then: 'Being mindful in the presence of cows.'

None of the Casta batted an eyelid. The solidity of their peaceful presence, so subtle and yet so very heavy at the same time, seemed to have impressed upon me the need to just be quiet, as they themselves are. Watching the thoughts come and go surrounded by such wily old masters of the trade can become as automatic as breathing in and out. Repeat: 'In *I* . . . out *AM,* in *I* . . . out *AM,*' and so on.

When I left the meadow a little later that evening, bathed in the glow of what felt like such a wonderful discovery, I was suddenly struck by the beauty of it all. Collared doves cooing softly in the background, a blackbird atop a swaying poplar singing the day to a close, and the Casta, of course, still sitting in their pure contentment, all combined to bring a deep feeling of privilege. I was grateful for having received such a perfect summing up of all that I felt in the company of the cows. It encapsulated everything I had felt before the filming began, but particularly during those exalted moments when the cameras were rolling.

Receiving such an unlooked-for gem stimulated a period of reflection, a looking back over the three and a half years since the first heifers had arrived on the farm. I reread articles that I'd written, dug out scraps of stories jotted down on the backs of old pieces of paper and revisited videos of the cows. I was curious to see if Cowfulness had always been there, tucked quietly away in the background. I'd known from the beginning that our farm was more about providing sanctuary than counting kilos of meat, yet I wanted to see if the writing reflected a mindful approach, even if I hadn't been consciously aware of it.

It didn't take long to find its fingerprints all over each and every text. It was so obvious that I smiled, laughing at my own lack of trust in what Life itself wanted to create on the farm. It even felt ridiculous to have thought that it could have been any other way. I was beginning to accept that mindfulness could become an incredibly powerful guiding force, shaping the life of anyone able to make a serious commitment to its practice. The deeper the determination to live mindfully, the more obvious the sense that there was a guiding hand taking care of one's daily affairs.

Without any conscious decision on my part, I had already been practising mindfulness for over twenty years before moving to the Pyrenees in 2014. For most of those years, I hadn't even heard of it, let alone tried to put it officially into practice. What I had done was spend hour after hour alone in nature, seeking quietness and calm among the trees and meadows and streams. Nowadays it might be called Forest Bathing or Forest Therapy. I craved the day when thoughts would be nothing more than clouds sailing through the blue of an endless sky. Being in nature seemed the best place to achieve this end; grass always seeming more friendly than glass or polished metal.

How then could I have begun raising the cattle in any other way? They were not to be exploited, but cherished. Their meat or milk would never feature on any annual balance sheet. It was I who would serve them. This much was clear before my brother's death through suicide. His passing only served to cement the bond between the bovine beauties and myself.

In retrospect, I could see that everything that had happened on the farm was first and foremost a reflection of the commitment to trying to live mindfully.

Approaching the cows in this way made decision-making and problem-solving a simple extension of attempting to live in the present moment. Rather than imposing my own thoughts and ideas on the cows, I had learned to listen to them, to just be among them and sense what they themselves were trying to tell me. This is common practice among those gifted individuals who have come to be known as horse whisperers. Why not with cows? Such intimacy still exists among certain African tribes who have turned cattle-raising into an art and form of worship. To a greater or lesser degree, cows are still considered to be sacred in India and the emergence over the last thirty years or so of farm sanctuaries in Europe and the USA testifies to the fact that, for many people, cows continue to be creatures deserving of our utmost respect and love. Cowfulness was all this converted into a single phrase that just happened to trip off the tongue quite nicely.

The final retreat of the season and all those that followed in 2019 only served to deepen my conviction that Cowfulness, and all it stood for, was for some people a very clear recipe for success. By success I mean being mindful, quietly turning within, learning to let go of the need to hold so very tightly to thoughts. I had the privilege of witnessing the transformation of some who arrived in difficulty and left light-footed and able to embrace all that Life had brought them.

The experience of one girl in particular touched me very deeply. She attended the yoga retreat in July 2019, and as I was to discover towards the end of our time together, came to the farm very much in the shadow of a very dark cloud. She had lost someone very close to her several years before – a car accident that took him from her in an instant – and since that moment all joy had drained away. The format of the retreats means that guests are rarely given official opportunities to share how they are feeling. The encouragement is simply to stay with whatever is going on, quietly watching all things come and go. Yet on the last day, she revealed that, miraculous as it seemed, and without having tried to do anything in particular, a thirst for living had returned and with it an acceptance that pain was never permanent, however endless it may feel at the time.

What she shared was absolute music to my ears and her

eyes on the morning of departure were a joy to behold – all shiny in celebration at the crossing of a difficult threshold. Thank you, Life, for these cows, who move mountains in their own unassuming way.

It seemed that the retreats were slowly but surely going from strength to strength. The cows had become very used to the presence of guests, and even though the BBC documentary hadn't led to a huge increase in visitors, they continued to come in a steady trickle.

However, even before Covid 19 arrived, just as the next season was beginning in March 2020, putting an enormous great spanner in the works, there was already one aspect of the Being with Cows gatherings that was proving to be a genuine thorn in the side. However hard we tried we just couldn't find an obvious solution. The problem was that we used the farmhouse to accommodate some of the guests during their stay (many also chose to camp, especially during the warmer months) and all meals were served in the dining room, with its beautiful view down the valley, stretching all the way to the Pyrenees themselves on the horizon.

The house itself had also played an important part in some guests' experiences on retreat. It was completely off-grid, made from natural materials such as straw bales, hemp and clay bricks made on site, and felt very much part of the land (as it actually was!), rather than something just sitting upon it. Many people had commented on how well they slept, cocooned as they felt in very simple rooms that transmitted a sense of staying within nature's bounds.

Yet for a week every month during the season, Diana

and the kids had to up sticks and either go to stay with her family in Spain or rent a small chalet on a local campsite, so that we could maximise the number of guests we could host in the house.

It wasn't ideal at all and led to a lot of friction between us at the time. Sustainably speaking, it just wasn't a long- or even medium-term solution. Even though our kids were being home-schooled during that period, it wasn't easy for them to integrate the monthly disruptions into what was already a very flimsy timetable. Their characters meant that they benefitted from a clear routine and the retreats quite often proved to undo all the foundation work that had been laid down in the weeks before each one began.

On one occasion, I'd entered such a quiet state by the end of the retreat that I clean forgot to go and collect Diana and the kids from the nearest train station 30km away. While Diana had been frantically trying to phone me, worried that my absence was due to some accident or the like, I was merrily wandering quietly among the cows. When they arrived back at the house by taxi later in the afternoon, I couldn't at first understand why they had returned in such a way. Diana, quite rightly, reminded me in no uncertain terms of the arrangements made before the retreat evicted them from what was their own house.

Such a situation couldn't continue. While I was able to dive deeply into retreat for several days each month, Diana's experience of the same period was one of increasing strain and anxiety. She fully supported the retreats, having been at my side throughout the fallout from Cork's suicide. She more than anyone else had witnessed the descent into despair and subsequent rising from the ashes in the company of the cows, and instinctively understood the deep source of support that I'd been blessed to tap into. All of this was clear, yet it was increasingly obvious that we couldn't continue as we were.

For a while we tried to figure out how we could accommodate guests on the farm without having to use the house, but every new idea led only to a series of dead ends. Visions of yurts (again) or pods or gypsy caravans came and went. Even the presence of two lovely wooden barns that came with the land, and which were already ripe for conversion, wasn't enough to convince us that the farm was somewhere we could continue to develop our project, a project which included not only the retreats but our family as a whole and, most importantly of all, the future wellbeing of our kids. Their position at the very top of the pyramid was unquestionable and any decision we made was in many ways made principally for them.

After weeks of discussion and debate, we just seemed to be going round in circles, chasing a tail that stubbornly refused to be caught. Eventually, rather than continue to bang our heads against an unyielding wall, we brought our eyes to rest on the last option on our list. Diana wrote a little note and hung it from the mirror inside the car. It was hard to accept at first after everything that had happened on the farm, especially since Cork passed on, but when we sat quietly with our dilemma in mind, trying our best to simply be with it, we would both come to the same conclusion. In a nutshell, it was time to move.

# CHAPTER II

# Pastures new

'Home is where you hear love within the stillness.'

RAQUEL FRANCO

Raulet. In the ancient language of the region, Occitan, it means 'reed' or 'place of reeds'. Occitan, though rarely spoken nowadays, was known in its time as a language of poetry, a romantic tongue favoured by troubadours and minstrels. The corner of south-western France in which we now live has recently been renamed Occitanie. It is a super-region, which previously consisted of the Midi Pyrenees and Languedoc-Roussillon. Languedoc refers to the language (*langue*) of the Occitan (*d'Oc*).

When I first came across the property for sale at Raulet in early May 2021, I began to get excited. I'd already been searching for months without success. Blurry eyed from so many hours sat at the computer, I was beginning to get a bit frustrated that nothing ticking the boxes on our list seemed available. It was a familiar story, for I remembered only too well the ups and downs experienced during the search that led us to Mirepoix several years before: too little or too much land; too close to a busy road; not enough grazing for the cows or simply out of the reach of our budget.

Something led me to start casting the net further afield and I began to look not only on farming or agricultural property websites, but also on those advertising terrain attractive to the hunting community – places that were rich in flora, fauna and biodiversity. Diana and I had already agreed that if we were to move from Mirepoix, it could only be to somewhere that locally might be described as being *bien preservé*. We wanted to move higher up, if we could, to a place where hills and the mountainous relief made cultivation a questionable venture, for we both loved woodland and wildflowers and hidden little hideaways where nature still ruled the roost – somewhere that could be said to be poetic in itself, reflective of the language and people that once populated the region many centuries ago.

It was on one such website that I came across a property that immediately piqued my interest: 100 hectares of deciduous woodland and wildflower meadow, a stream and an average altitude of around 675 metres. Not the mountains themselves, but much closer, and high enough up to remain relatively fresh, especially at night, when the inevitable heat settled over the landscape in summer.

What's more, the sale included a beautiful old stone farmhouse with attached barns and outbuildings, a small bungalow with glorious views across the valley, and, most interesting of all, a steel-framed barn which had been partly converted into holiday accommodation. The farm had once hosted parties of pony trekkers and the facilities were thus already designed with groups in mind.

As I pinged back and forth between the pages of the online advert, a very similar feeling to one I had experienced when we first discovered the farm at Mirepoix began to surface. The clearest indication of this was a slowing down of all thoughts, very much like when I was with the cows. I had learned to trust those moments when speculative thinking was absent and this was very much one of those occasions. Rather than commence another habitual round of yes-no-yes-no imagined projections onto the property, I just sat quietly and enjoyed the feeling of *possibility*.

The following afternoon, we made what might be called our first contact with the land at Raulet. I'd spoken with the estate agent to arrange a visit, but overcome with excited impatience and with the kids still at school I bundled Diana into the car and set off. Even though it was only 20km away from Mirepoix, we soon discovered a very different landscape to the one we had called home for the past years. The higher we climbed, the patchwork of dry scrubby woodland and fields of wheat and maize gave way to great stands of beech and beautiful wildflower meadows. Villages and hamlets were noticeable by their absence and there was a distinct sense of being just that few centimetres more off the map.

Even before reaching the property itself, I could feel a great big YES welling up inside me. I didn't say anything to Diana, as I had the habit of blurting out all sorts of gibberish when something got hold of me, but as virtually all trace of human activity dropped away, I just knew that we were heading towards what would become our future home. I couldn't explain it but that sense of knowing was something that came from somewhere far wiser and knowledgeable than everyday Dave could ever claim to be.

The narrow little lane petered out at the door to the old farmhouse and in some intuitive way, I was already interpreting the property as somehow representing the end of the road. Everything, it seemed, could stop here.

As we walked up the forest track that wound its way through the main valley to the highest point of the land, this impression of bringing things to a conclusion got steadily stronger. Even the buzzing swarm of thoughts that attempted to insist their way into awareness could do nothing to disturb the feeling of having arrived home. I wasn't experiencing any sense of déjà vu or familiarity with the landscape, but the whole thing spoke of a rare kind of quietness that I'd occasionally felt with the cows – those so-called peak moments when living becomes being and nothing more. Everything was still: the birds were busy chattering away and a healthy breeze ruffled the tops of the green-again trees, yet all was undeniably quiet, and in some way, unmoving.

A week later we returned with the kids to explore a bit more. I wanted to look at the stream that tumbled down from the crest of the highest hills. Water in a seasonally dry landscape is a very precious resource for many reasons: psychologically, it offers a sense of freshness and fertility and encourages a feeling of confidence and continuation; for downright fun, there's nothing better than splashing around in cool water in the midst of yet another record-breaking heatwave and, practically speaking, I wanted to see if there was enough flow to support the cows through what are becoming increasingly dry summers.

What we discovered that afternoon was an absolute delight for us all. Over the course of its long history, the stream had carved out a series of ravines and moss-covered gullies, so dripping with atmosphere that even the kids were hushed into frequent bouts of silence. As it twisted and turned down the valley, it had worn away the limestone bed in certain places so that natural hollows had been formed, deep cool basins of crystal-clear water. The waterfalls that cascaded down over the steepest sections had gouged out pools that were deep enough to swim in, which had the boys in their excitement already pulling off shoes and socks to paddle.

While Gabi, Elie and I were busy counting newts in one of the pools, Diana slunk quietly away to wander a while in the forest. When she returned an hour later, her face was a picture of contentment. She told us that at some point in her walk, she'd sat down to rest against the trunk of a big beech. A few minutes passed before she heard a slight rustling up above her on the slope. And then, to her amazement, a roe deer, a doe from what she described, trotted gently down the hill towards her. She said it showed no fear, was in no hurry to bolt away as is sadly the norm on such occasions, but carried on browsing and nibbling on the flush of newly opened leaves.

The encounter had already charmed Diana, whose back catalogue of such experiences in her native Barcelona amounted to the grand total of zero. When, a short time later, a fox padded its way along a trail in front of her, she said that she too, enraptured by such contact with what were to become our closest neighbours, felt a very distinct sense of homecoming. Good: we were in agreement then. No need to look any further. Everything ended here.

We returned several times to Raulet over the course of the next heat-hazed months and each visit only served to deepen our conviction that here was a place where all aspects of the project could take root and flourish. The holiday accommodation and barn it was contained in could all be converted into a dedicated retreat centre, a place where guests could be hosted in ecologically designed comfort. No need for Diana and the kids to trundle off to Spain once a month, an increasingly difficult prospect seeing as the boys were now happily installed at the local gem of a primary school just a five-minute drive from the farm.

The old stone farmhouse was in need of quite serious amounts of renovation, yet the small bungalow higher up at the entrance to the property could provide us with a place to stay while the works were being done.

There was even a natural spring on the land, separate from the stream itself — a pure source of high-quality water that continued to bubble and flow year-round, albeit at a trickle during the summer and early autumn.

And as for the cows, well, the forty or so hectares of

wildflower meadow, such a rich mixture of ancient grasses and medicine-making herbs was enough to have even myself slavering at the mouth. In fact the kids, used as they were to being surrounded by the cows, would often ape their extended family and get stuck into some clover or sweet-tasting grass stems.

All the criteria that had formed part of our initial search had been well and truly met in the wooded folds of this magnificent hidden valley. We couldn't have asked for more. The fear of some kind of hidden catch rearing its ugly head, which indeed we had in abundance during the negotiations to purchase the property, simply provided us with more opportunities to deepen our commitment to living mindfully. In fact, it was this that underpinned the whole move – the desire to dive deeper and deeper into what Ramana Maharshi often referred to as '*Just being quiet.*' It was both inescapable and inevitable that the upping of sticks was but a reflection of the unspoken vow that Diana and I had made, a pledge to sacrifice what we *thought* of as ourselves to the greater good, and by that I mean the truest representation of our authentic being – what I simply like to call the heart.

During the autumn of 2021, in those moments when it seemed like the whole deal was about to be skittled by one thing or another, I realised with even greater force that the move was nothing about the satisfying of so many desires that I carried around with me, even if they appeared on the surface to be honourable or motivated by a wish to do things in the name of peace. It was, quite simply, about *letting go*. Every single time I set foot on the land there during those cold and often rain-soaked days, I experienced what appeared to be a conflicting mix of sheer delight at having found it *and* dread that the place could be plucked out of our very hands, snatched away just when we seemed to have found the perfect place to live.

What to do? Let go, that's what. Both Diana and myself eventually sighed our way into acceptance of whatever would be would be. Over and over again, the Maharshi's words reminded us that surrender, scary as it may seem at first, was the only real option. The desire to control the situation, to quicken or even force the sale by one means or another, only ever led to frustration.

I can't say specifically at what point the penny dropped and I clearly understood the necessity of taking the hands off the reins, but once it had been taken onboard, things proceeded both more smoothly and swiftly than before.

Yes, there were still reactions during those moments when we felt beaten down by yet another seemingly trivial delay, but as soon as we remembered that the sun, shining high above those darkened banks of cloud, would continue to shine regardless of our emotional protests, everything was suddenly OK, exactly as it was.

The cows were a continued reminder of all this. In the first blustery days of winter, then stretching out into the New Year (the weeks leading up to the signing of the first contract) several of the Casta mothers gave birth. Each new precious bundle of legs and dewy-eyed inno-cence put the whole situation into a very grounded, earthy perspective. One look in their impossibly shiny eyes, alive with arrival and wonder, made any anxiety about the purchase of Raulet seem no more important than a most temporary and fleeting case of hiccups.

One of the calves, in particular, drove all this home in a stark and almost painful way. I knew that her mum Llorelie was ready to calve, and the normal policy for births during the colder months was to get the mother into the barn and out of any weather. However, try as I might, Llorelie's innate Casta stubbornness meant that I just couldn't get her in. Whatever will be will be. A couple of days after making the final attempt, I went up early in the morning to check on the herd and top up their hay when I saw Llorelie lying down right next to the fence, the great wad that is a cow's afterbirth glistening pink in the sun beside her. The calf was nowhere to be seen. In summer this would have been completely normal. Like the red and roe deer hinds they share the land with, the Casta mothers hide their newborn for the first few days of its life. It's a natural instinct still prevalent among very ancient and rustic breeds who give birth in woodland or scrub or rough meadow. They can lead you a merry dance, distracting, feigning illness or even injury at times in a bid to lure you away from their little one.

Llorelie and the rest of the herd, however, were at this time confined to their winter quarters – a large paddock and open-fronted wooden barn where they could go to feed and sit out any storms. While there was a small patch of woodland by the barn, there was nowhere she could have hidden her calf. It was only when I went back to her to see if her eyes could point me in the right direction that I saw one strand of the fencing wire behind her had come undone. I immediately looked down the small slope beyond and there at the bottom, curled up in a shivering ball was her calf, all covered in muck and seemingly mystified by such a tough start to her little life. I knew that she'd been born several hours before as her coat was perfectly dry, but she was so weak that she couldn't stand. The first priority was to get her up and into the barn, where I could have a proper look at her.

That done, she got a vigorous rubbing down with straw, an attempt to mimic the rough, stimulating massage that the mother performs with her tongue, reaffirming the physicality of the world into which her calf has been born. When Sylvia, as the little one had been named, had stopped shivering, she was carried out into the yard to be with her mama. Bewildered perhaps by what had become something of a drama, her mother did the most un-Casta-like thing I had ever witnessed and ran away into the trees. Normally so deeply maternal and protective of their young, it was a shock to see Llorelie behaving in such a way. After calling her several times, gently trying to bring her in with a stream of soothing words, I left Sylvia curled up in a pile of leaves and retreated to the far side of the park, trusting that with me out of the way, her mother's instincts would take over and all would be well, as it had been with every Casta calf born so far on the farm.

When an hour later the hoped-for reunion still hadn't happened, I whizzed off to the vets in Mirepoix to get a tube of colostrum, the crucial feed each calf receives in the first few wobbly moments of its life.

By midday, I was still sat with Sylvia in the barn, her tiny little elfin head resting in my lap. She was warm, well fed after the colostrum and most of a bottle of powdered milk, and as far as I could see, out of any danger. Leaving her to sleep, I returned to the house to be greeted by the news that there was to be yet another delay in the purchase of Raulet. The latest rendezvous had been cancelled due to some unforeseen technical hitch. Rewind a year or so and the same situation may have seen an impatient tantrum brewing up on my horizon. Now, in light of Sylvia's struggles that morning and the constant reminder the cows were giving on a daily basis, the delay was accepted as nothing more than so much background noise, a little annoying at first but ultimately not worthy of any further attention.

Mindfulness can help molehills remain as molehills. The helter-skelter ride that comes when we harness ourselves to our thoughts is what makes them into mountains. When I saw Sylvia that evening curled up asleep in the hay under the watchful gaze of her mother, the last remaining lumps of frustration crumbled away – no molehills, no mountains, just an exceptionally tender scene that had cowfulness written all over it. For a moment I sat down and cried. Not with relief but gratitude, the weight of which brought tears pouring out of my eyes. The calf, the cows, the move to Raulet and everything it offered, all seemed so impossible in the aftermath of Corky's death, that now that it really appeared to be happening, I experienced such a depth of gratefulness that I couldn't help but weep. Tragedy doesn't have to become a lifelong trauma and the Corky I saw as I looked out across the cows was not a pitiful figure at all but a shining light of inspiration, a brother still and more so now that he had lit up the path ahead.

I did succumb a while later to a deep sense of sadness, wishing with all my heart that he was sat by my side, that I could have shown him the farm, the cows, the kids, especially the kids, who I'm sure would have adored their silly Uncle Cork. One look at little Sylvia, however, stopped such thoughts dead in their tracks. He *is* here, she seemed to say, in every possible way; more than you can ever imagine.

And to think that *I* was the one who was supposed to be looking after the cows!

The *compromis de vente* was signed without any great fuss in the end, towards the close of February 2022. This document signifies the first part of the purchase, to be followed upon completion by the *Acte*. We were, it seems, finally on our way.

By the end of March 2022, we had just a further month to wait before finally moving to Raulet. Spring had most definitely sprung in the foothills of the French Pyrenees. There were cowslips and celandines and lungwort aplenty lining the roadside verges. Chiffchaffs and cuckoos had arrived from Africa and were busy singing out their names in every patch of woodland. The frogs had tentatively made an odd croak or two and strong easterly gales had stripped the last of the curled old leaves from the trees.

There was the beginning of warmth and the cows could

sense the coming flush of fresh green grass. They were already out on the land, the calves cavorting from here to there and back again. Two more Casta mothers were ready to calve and the Galloways, already shedding their outer coats after an exceptionally mild winter, were as relaxed and unassuming as only they can be. They already knew about the coming move – I'd told them time and again that there's this place up in the hills, such a place of springs and streams and acre upon acre of meadow. There's woodland, too, great goliaths of oak and beech and chestnut, standing guard over a land that is nothing short of a paradise. When I told them such things, I knew they understood. Their lack of reaction is exactly why I love them so very much.

They know it was for them that the whole idea of moving gathered pace in the first place; everything that has followed trails only in their wake. The well-worn path they have blazed through the thorny scrub of our own inner landscapes has led us, screaming and kicking at times, to a place of increasingly quiet resilience (when the kids are asleep at least). Cowfulness is not some Instagram-inspired marketing gimmick but the absolute rock upon which the whole farm is founded.

The potential of cows to give birth not only to their calves, but also in unknown ways to life-affirming projects, is a little-known secret that awaits wider discovery. While wondering how to bring this book to its natural conclusion, I was drawn to reread David Godman's excellent book dedicated to the life and teachings of Ramana Maharshi – *The Power of the Presence*. I was especially captivated by a passage in the chapter devoted to the cow Lakshmi. It details the building of an unusually extravagant and expensive cowshed, much out of keeping with the normally frugal approach to the management of the ashram's finances as overseen by the Maharshi. In the words of one devotee, Annamalai Swami:

'Chinnaswami had made an arrangement with a local mason to build a small cowshed that would cost not more than Rs 500. Bhagavan (the Maharshi) wanted a bigger cowshed:

"Many cows will come here in the next few years," he said. "Even if we build a big cowshed, there will be so many cows that some of them will have to be kept outside. We must make a larger cowshed and you, rather than this mason, must supervise its construction."

Once, as we were supervising the work together, Bhagavan told me, "If you build this cowshed for Lakshmi, we will get all the necessary *punya* [merit or good karma that accrues from performing virtuous acts] to build a bookstore, a dining room and a shrine for the mother. All this will happen in due course. This will eventually become a town."[2]

The construction of the cowshed marked a turning point in the ashram's history. Prior to its construction,

2 Sri Annamalai Swami *Living By The Words Of Bhagavan*, pp. 46–7, 53.

ashram buildings were generally small and primitive. In the years that followed many new granite buildings were constructed: the ashram office, the *Veda Patasala* (a school dedicated to the chanting of holy vedic scripture), the kitchen and dining room, and finally the magnificent temple erected over the *Samadhi* (memorial shrine) of Bhagavan's mother. Along with the growth of these physical structures there was a corresponding increase in the flow of visitors to the ashram. Was there really a connection between Bhagavan's decision to build this cowshed and the huge growth that followed? It may appear to be a strange claim, but when Lakshmi passed away in 1948, Bhagavan himself commented, "Because of her our family has grown to this extent".[3]

The joy that came bubbling up as I read these words was linked, I felt, to the fact that they described something very similar to my experiences here in south-western France. The lowest common denominator in all our comings and goings is the cows. Though so often such an unseen presence, tucked away in the woods or hilly meadows, they lie at the very epicentre of both the farm and our family life. While we bounce from one thing to another, there they truly are, unwaveringly still and silent.

Of course I am biased. How can I not be when they heaved me out of that darkened hole in the days and weeks following Cork's passing? In the eight or so years

3 Godman, David *The Power and the Presence 3* pp. 280–3.

since those little heifers first set foot on the farm, they have insisted I follow their lead. Their refusal to accept anything other than a steadfast dedication to quietness has brought me face-to-face with all that I am not. So many things that are surplus to requirements have, in their presence, just fallen away. An innate sense of natural humility, which is their daily bread and butter, has relentlessly exposed every false refuge into which I've tried to crawl. They simply won't have it. One glance, the merest brush with those unblinking eyes is enough; quietness is king and among those whose inner compass points always to harmony, such calm is deeply infectious.

# CHAPTER 12

# Thank you

'Gratitude is not only the greatest of virtues but the parent of all the others.'

MARCUS TULLIUS CICERO

We finally moved to Raulet on the 29 April 2022. It was a deliciously cool, misty and perfectly atmospheric evening. By 8pm, it was fresh enough to warrant lighting the beautiful wood burner that came with the house.

The kids were in high spirits, already eager to explore their new kingdom, even in the half-light of dusk.

The dogs were champing at the bit to go off exploring too, especially Mila, our young lurcher, who I'm sure suddenly realised that she had arrived in paradise.

Diana's face wore a rosy glow, her eyes an are-we-really-here? look, glinting softly in the firelight.

I have to admit, I pinched myself a few times too, just to make sure. Before the light had been totally snuffed out by the mist, I took a few minutes to gaze out across the sloping meadows in front of the house. Something caught my eye, way up on the furthest patch of grass; out of the woodland came three *chevreuil*, a roe deer doe and what looked like two of her young from the year before. If I needed any confirmation that we'd come to a good place, this was it.

The next evening, another misty affair of cloud and gentle breeze, was when I really felt that the move had become a concrete reality and not something that continually lingered in the realm of thought. Why? Well, it was when the first cows arrived at their new home. The day had been spent ferrying stuff from Mirepoix to the new HQ and even though I'd just about had enough by the time evening came, an idea crept into the mind that it would be good to bring just one load of the Casta back home with us.

They had already been brought down to the barn in readiness for the move and within twenty minutes, Pellie, Petou, Qupe and little Rodi, all the male members of the herd, were safely in the trailer and ready to go. Normally speaking, loading even one Casta into the stock box can be something of an event, often involving an hour or more of patient, inch by inch movements, a rich catalogue of what you might call colourful language and the straining of muscle and sinew.

This time, the whole lot walked on without a care in the world. I took it as another great sign and set off for the hills, hoping to arrive before the darkness overtook us. A murky, moisture-laden twilight greeted their first footsteps on the land at Raulet, their hooves carving through the wet grass to leave silver-shining trails in their wake.

Within minutes, however, the grand arrival had become something of a farce, as Pellie, swiftly followed by the others, went straight through the newly installed fencing and promptly disappeared into the mist. GREAT! The rest of the 100 hectares was unfenced. It was almost a new moon and even when the mist and cloud parted for a few seconds, all I could make out were their pale backsides galloping across another field into the nearest pocket of woodland.

'PELLIE!!!' My voice echoed around the valley, bouncing back from the wall of trees newly covered in leaf.

What was that about mindfulness? I returned to the house muttering a host of choice words under my breath and swore that I wanted nothing to do with Casta ever again. At first light the next morning, the large meadow in front of the house bore evidence of their nocturnal ramblings. In every direction there lay trails of flattened grass where they had explored their new landscape. I shouted and hollered, hoping to call them back down into the bottom of the valley and the fenced meadow from which they had escaped, but all to no avail. Masters at minding their own business, they remained quite perfectly hidden, tucked away in some patch of woodland where I just couldn't find them.

With the rest of the Casta still waiting to be carried from Mirepoix and the Galloways too, I couldn't spend the morning trying to track them down. All that could be done, like so many times before, was to trust that whatever would be would be and accept that any amount of fussing or clucking around like an old hen would contribute absolutely nothing beneficial whatsoever to any attempt to get them back.

When the next load of Casta arrived at Raulet a couple of hours later, their excited calls as they set foot on the land for the first time soon had Pellie and the rest careering down the scrubby slopes to be reunited with at least some of the herd they'd left behind the day before. I didn't even need to open the gate or take down any of the electric fence, for they sailed straight over the wire in their haste to sniff and lick and gently lock horns with some of their extended family once more.

By late afternoon all of the Casta had been safely carried to their new home, and wonderfully happy they seemed too. As normal, once they were all back together, they spent a good half hour charging round the meadow in what for them amounted to almost utter abandon. Right from the smallest calves to the oldest cows, the whole herd kicked and bucked and threw their heads high, casting off for once their reserve and keep-it-all-in countenance, revelling in the sheer delight of being somewhere new, somewhere that so obviously felt so very good indeed.

By the following evening, the Galloways too had been ferried from Mirepoix and as far as I was concerned, the move was complete. Yes, there was still a mass of stuff to be fetched from Petite Fournet, which eventually took more than a month to sort out, yet having *them* among us again, seeing their hoof-prints pressed deep into the rich and giving earth, was enough for me.

Beyond thrilled might come a tiny bit close to describing the feeling I experienced during those first misty days at Raulet. There was grass aplenty for the cows, the likes of which I had never seen, even at the very height of spring in Mirepoix. Not only grass but an incredible abundance of wildflowers. So beautiful did the meadows look that I was even reluctant to let the cows on them at first. The great mass of orchids, bedstraws and richly assorted members of the clover family were living, colourful splashes of meditation, stunning enough to turn visual feast into an inner song of gratitude.

And so it continued. The first few months of life at Raulet sped by not in a blur but a rich kaleidoscope of seasonal delights. The cows grew fat like I'd never seen them before, the Galloways bringing three new bundles of furry perfection into our lives. Such was the abundance of their mothers' milk that the calves grew at a pace that genuinely surprised me. The Casta meanwhile were transformed into rounded, meaty versions of their previous selves. They are not traditionally known as a beef breed, their angular shape more aligned with milking cattle. Yet now before my almost disbelieving eyes, they filled out tremendously, shining in their newly found plumpness.

As they rotated from meadow to woodland and back again, I think we all revelled in the fact that there was always something fresh and green to eat, be it grass and herbs that continued to grow despite being heavily grazed or nourishing leaves from the wide variety of trees that covered most of the land. Such a situation felt nothing short of luxurious.

Back in Mirepoix, it was lucky if the cows could graze well for three months of the year. The rest of the time they ate hay or alfalfa. Here, suddenly, there was greenery a plenty to keep a smile on all our faces.

This all changed, however, as late spring gave way to summer. During May and most of June, the exceptionally high temperatures were tempered a little by several good rainstorms. Watered by these welcome downpours, the land remained vibrant and capable of supporting several flushes of fresh grass. Come July, this vital source of refreshing moisture simply ceased to exist. Wave after wave of unrelenting heat swiftly removed all trace of fertility from the land. The streams and all other water courses dried up within weeks. Even the two springs that had historically continued to flow year-round gave up the ghost and retired deep within the earth.

Deciduous trees shed their leaves in an effort to conserve water. Great swathes of softwoods, douglas and sitka spruce mainly, simply shrivelled up and died. At 700 metres above sea level, we fared better than some of the other farms further down the valley. The nearest town to us, Limoux, 600 dusty metres lower, reminded me of some of the parched, arid landscapes I'd travelled through in Morocco several years before.

The summer storms, great thundering affairs that lit up the night skies for hours at a time, simply never arrived. In the less hilly parts of the area, entire fields of maize were left to die, thousands of tonnes just withering away on the stalks. Irrigation was officially forbidden and Lac de Montbel, the nearest freshwater reservoir to us, became nothing more than a puddle.

Such a prolonged spell of unbroken dryness did have its benefits, however. For roughly three months, Gabi and myself slept out under the stars every night. What a relief it was to stretch out at the end of yet another scorching day. Raulet is fortunate enough to be free of the kind of light pollution that has become a blight in many other parts of the world. Almost all of the major constellations that are visible from this part of Europe can be seen in wonderful detail.

Shooting stars could be observed in their entirety and Gabi delighted in following the dot-sized satellites in orbit round the earth. We were serenaded by crickets and the few cicadas who made home high up in these hills and even the harsh sound of barking roe deer became a kind of lullaby soothing us into sleep.

On several occasions during this period, with the drought seeming to squeeze the very life out of the land-scape, we dropped down to Mirepoix for one thing or another. If I thought things were difficult high up at Raulet, one look at the frazzled what-had-been fields surrounding the picturesque little town brought tears to my eyes. The land wasn't even yellow or brown anymore, but a lifeless looking grey and increasingly so as the rain-less days continued.

At our new home, the cows had stayed well by becoming browsers again, forced by the exceptional heat to seek shelter in the woodland, the leaves of which kept them fat and well nourished. Down in the lowlands, the flatter areas surrounding towns like Mirepoix, some of the herds of farmers that I knew had become but shadows of their former selves.

It was on the way back from one such visit that I experienced a sudden and very profound sense of gratitude. It welled up inside me as a bubbling spring of gratefulness, cool and crystal clear. My eyes misted over again. How was it I could feel so held in the midst of what had become, for many farmers at least, a genuine crisis? My attention came to rest on the move from Mirepoix. At the very moment that the worst drought in living and recorded memory had sucked most parts of France dry, life had moved us up into the hills, to catch the morning dew and freshening breeze. The cows, those four-legged family members whose well-being lay behind the upping of sticks, had been provided for. We too had been taken care of, sheltered under the unseen wing of something beyond all thought.

Who was it that took us out of an off-grid house that relied on rainfall for its water, away from a land where the heavy clay became like cracked concrete even during an averagely warm summer? What invisible hand had scooped us all up and gently dropped us at the feet of the mountains, uplifted by such absolute generosity?

As we climbed back up towards Raulet, the appreciation of what felt like a clear case of divine intervention deepened into an acknowledgement that our entire lives, every mysterious millisecond and apparent action, can only ever be attributed to the workings of what some may call the Supreme. We have no influence whatsoever over what we mistakenly call our lives, we just *think* we do. And this is the very heart of the matter, the very foundation of mindfulness and all methods and teachings that purport to point the way home.

Ramana Maharshi repeatedly stated that for those unable to shed their egoic skin in his presence, there existed but two routes to salvation: self-enquiry or devotional self-surrender — a laying of one's very existence at the feet of the Lord. Although he appeared to favour self-enquiry as the foremost of the two paths, he admitted that they were both rivers to the same sea.

Since Cork's death I had submerged myself in the waters of both streams, trusting that ultimately, they were one and the same. This gratitude that had me so gripped on the way home from Mirepoix stripped away all sense of self-identity for a while. In such a rarefied atmosphere, it was obvious in a most beautifully tender way that the two techniques were loving proof of an indescribably caring and benevolent presence. That lifelines as these existed at all were heartfully accepted as an undoubted sign of Life's unending compassion.

Later that evening, while checking in with the Casta, this whole understanding deepened further. Rishi, a young heifer who had been named with Ramana in mind, slowly wandered over for her daily scratch. As we stood together in the fading light, I realised that I had never been who I thought I was. An image came of standing in front of a mirror, seeing the figure that I had long been persuaded was the real me. Something suddenly wanted verification. Where was the proof? Had anyone ever even raised the subject, questioned the validity of what was now seen as an incredibly convincing imposter?

Laughter bubbled up, followed by a stream of words: squatter; charlatan; swindler; fraud. The person who never had been became nothing more than a fleeting image projected upon some unknown screen. Rishi, however, seemed to have assumed a position of great elevation. Her eyes sparkled, the light of a dying sun reflected amber in their depths. She appeared to be undeniably real, singing from a more naturally mindful and present hymn sheet than my so-called ordinary self.

For several moments, I basked in the glory of utter thoughtlessness, a total absence of thinking. It's not that there were great feelings of bliss, nor any sense of quietness at all; everything just felt so perfectly normal and *ordinary*. Then came understanding: it's always like this beneath the veneer of mental grime. When the windows are cleaned, the light comes shining through, pouring its formless Self into this great ocean of simplicity.

There's nothing that can be done, nowhere to go without it ever being the work of Life itself. Its fingerprints are over everything. Yes, its touch may seem cold, callous even and at times so painfully far beyond cruel. Yet as I looked once again at Rishi, even suffering could be seen as evidence of Life's unquestionable grace and love.

What had happened with Cork had brought an almost unbearable slab of grief and pain crashing down on our entire family. Crushed beneath the choking weight of rubble, we wriggled our way out to an apparent place of acceptable safety. I cannot speak for Mum and Dad, for Pete or any of the rest but up there on that wooded hillside, at perfect ease in the company of a regal-looking Rishi, it was clear that suffering is Life's way of quickening the homeward journey. Whatever form it may take, the pressure, the loneliness, the aching desire to feel part of something meaningful, is perfectly designed to point one in the only valid direction. What may be a gentle but explosive nudge for some can be a most difficult and even crucifying movement for others, an oft-repeated drawn-out saga that seems to have no end. Yet every shove in the back and shuddering kick in the ribs is but Life's way of leading one within, of twisting and turning attention back to the seat of authentic being.

Pain becomes purposeful, not a barrier or even something to be overcome. It is the dry kindling that feeds the flames of remembrance, a recall of Life's all-inclusive totality. What follows in its wake is not the stuff of words but of deep determined action, resilience and a steadfast commitment to trust. Gratitude is a refusal to bow down to the restless traffic of thought that circulates *sans pause* but for brief moments of calm. Taking the hands off the wheel can be terrifying at times, yet there comes a moment, a lightning flash of realisation, when it is seen that one was never in actual control in the first place. Oh what a blessed relief! What luxury. To be driven and not have to drive. In the same vein, Ramana talked of the folly of the person who catches a train but continues to carry their baggage on their back. Put it down, for God's sake. Unburden yourself of the idea of personal involvement.

The climax of this peep behind the curtain came as Rishi turned away to join her mother Lotus and the rest of the herd. Watching them disappear into the undergrowth, the reference point habitually referred to as me simply ceased to exist. What sang out loud and clear in its absence was this: there is no-one else; there are no others; there is only Life itself as one inseparable undivided whole. The Casta, who had by now cracked their way over fallen trunks and branches further into the woodland, were not outside me at all, for they too in all and absolute simplicity, had no definable existence to call their own. Everything, everywhere, in every apparent direction could only ever be Life. There is, thankfully, no escape. It was all so clear while it lasted, as too was the understanding that commitment to realising this inner flowering is the sole meaningful aim of one's life. Everything else pales into insignificance.

Threading my way back down the hillside, the sense of gratitude returned, washing in with the evening dew. The clucking of several blackbirds announced that the resident tawny owls were out and about and somewhere far off came the earthy sound of wild boar grunting and grumbling their way through the woods. Cocooned as I still was in the quietness, I accepted all I was experiencing as simply being part of myself, neither outside nor in, just Life and nothing more. I could say that for once there was real happiness, a joy without cause or reason which underpinned the gratefulness.

On reaching the bottom of the valley, I sought out the Galloways. Clustered round the metal hay feeder, they hardly looked up as I approached. I smiled as I passed by, pausing only to stroke the ever-available Orion. There was such a comical look on his face that I laughed out loud, chuckling away at the warm perfection of it all, just being with cows.

# Epilogue

Arriving at the feeders where the Casta were already gathered, I noticed that the remaining leaves on the trees seemed to be infused with an extra intensity, that their colours were somehow warmer and less sharply defined than normal.

The whole scene in fact brought a smile to the face: the cows were looking magnificent in the autumnal light. The jostling for position ahead of the topping up of the hay seemed to be more of a dance than an attempt to establish domination.

As it is their habit, several of them stood directly in front of the feeder that I wanted to refill. They have no fear whatsoever of the tractor and all the mechanical disturbance it brings into their midst and, as normal, it took a very gentle pushing of the rear ends with the bale itself to shift them out of the way.

That done, I jumped down from the tractor to lower the roof of the feeder to the floor. The whole thing, as functional as it is, is a homemade affair that has for a roof several sheets of corrugated iron fixed into a half moon shape to keep the rain off the hay. Lowering the roof to the ground on one side of the feeder so that the round bale could be dropped inside involves removing two bolts from metal support bars that normally serve to keep the roof upright and in place. I'd done the very same thing over and over throughout the previous months, yet crucially on this occasion, I forgot to attach the safety rope that prevented the roof from sliding to the floor in one powerful movement once the bolts have been removed.

Life alone knows how such apparent forgetfulness could so penetrate and disturb what had become a very carefully executed routine. I knew that the roof was not the safest design, and that without the necessary levels of concentration, it could even become a hazard when moved. It weighed a couple of hundred kilos at least. Such thoughts, however, had always been with the cows in mind. I had been concerned that it could, without careful handling, come down onto one of the beauties, trapping a head or two inside.

Never in my wildest dreams did I ever envisage that it could be me who became a victim of its homemade unpredictability. That rope! Its untied and flapping form bouncing against the metal bars in the freezing December wind. It's funny how the very thing that would lead me down into such desperation would prove to be a saviour of sorts, in what rapidly became a dreadfully difficult situation.

Clang. It doesn't seem much when written down on paper. Just a few letters, really, gathered together in some onomatopoeic order. Play around with it for a while, its base but simple solidity rolling quite comfortably off the tongue. Clang!

And so it was that the trap was set. Life, the heart as Hunter, ensnaring its prey between bars of unforgiving iron. As soon as the remaining bolt was removed, the roof slammed down at breakneck speed, trapping my left arm between the pincer-like metal supports. Disbelief. Disbelief and an instantaneous sense of dread. Pain, the like of which I have never experienced before, seared burning hot from the hand up to the armpit, surfing a tsunami of nervous overload. The tension exerted by the weight of the roof was so great and the pressure so immense that most of the fingers were immediately pulled into what seemed like impossibly grotesque shapes.

How long is a second really? It can be measured, sure, but when time is so compressed by the sheer enormity of the situation, such as I the one I suddenly found myself in, it moves into a realm of poorly defined limits.

At first came panic and disbelief, a refusal to accept both the situation itself and its undoubted severity.

I was more than a kilometre away from the house, tucked away in the wooded fold of a valley. It was cold, freezing cold and the sun had already dipped down behind the shoulders of the tree-clad hills. This luxury of non-acceptance was soon squeezed out of its own skin as the true gravity of the situation dawned on me.

In one unshakeably crystallised moment, it seemed that everything that I had ever preached about mindfulness, acceptance and trust in life had to be put into the most immediate and unwavering practice.

'It's okay, it's okay,' I whispered to myself and then, 'Breathe, you can do it.' Every single ounce of attention that I could summon up from the depths was directed towards one vital end — escape. Acceptance definitely didn't mean laying down to die, freezing to death to be found countless hours later as a tattered rag of a human being still trapped between the bars. I genuinely felt as if I needed to fight, with all the strengths I possessed, not only for the arm, but perhaps for my life itself.

This will to survive manifested at first as an attempt to lift the roof by way of pulling on its nearest point. I could reach without difficulty the support bars that kept the sheeted iron in place, but try as I might, I could only lift the heavy mass at most a couple of centimetres. It wasn't enough and to make matters worse, the relief that flooded the entire length of my crumpled arm became an almost unbearable torture as the full weight of all that metal settled down on it again.

For minutes that felt like endless hours, I pushed and pulled, grunting with the effort, guttural noises from deep down that were absorbed by the surrounding trees. Panic welled up again and, yes, I thought that I was destined to die there, the flame slowly snuffed out by a combination of pain and sub-zero temperatures. I prayed that redemption would come in the form of a hunter or another local wandering through the woods in search of mushrooms. It simply wasn't meant to be. I even prayed that one of the Casta, most of whom stood not five metres from my side, would come and lift up the roof with a single nudge of the head.

# Epilogue

What they actually did was to continue to stare, placidly chewing the cud, not in the least bit concerned, it seemed, at my desperate attempts to escape. I begged Pellie to come, to turn trauma into the miraculous with a single swish of his great head, but he just looked at me impassively, those great unblinking eyes unaffected by my plight.

I don't know how many minutes had passed since I had become trapped. I was beginning to experience a new wave of desperation. It resurfaced like some great immovable block of ice, cold and unconcerned. Again and again, I wrestled with the roof bars, moving them enough to release the pressure, but never the arm itself. Tiredness began to creep in and with it, for the first time, a sense of dreadful inevitability. Acceptance? Maybe not. More of a kind of withering resignation. Try as I might, I just couldn't see any way out.

I started to shiver and my mouth became so dry that I couldn't even muster enough saliva to spit. I had kicked my wellies off earlier, a forlorn attempt to block the bars with their steel-toe-capped solidity, but every effort had resulted in them slipping onto the floor. My socks were caked in mud and cow muck and their pitiful state seemed to sum up exactly how I was feeling during those disturbing moments.

It was then that I started to shout, screaming for someone to help me. There are virtually endless mantras in existence, sacred words and phrases of liberation. Some are as old as the world itself. 'Help' is not normally considered to be among them, not in Sanskrit, Hindi, or any other ancient tongue. Down there, though, in that pit of raw emotion, it roared out of my mouth like the bellowing of some wild Scottish stag held fast in the grip of a claggy mountain bog. Everything I had went into those shouted pleas for help, but the longer they continued, the more I felt that they were only serving to drain me of what energy I had left.

After such full-throated efforts, the silence and quietness that followed was quite deafening, and for a moment it permitted no thought. Momentarily released from the necessity of thinking about what to do, I instinctively began talking to my trapped hand, soothing it with both gentle words and soft massaging strokes from the other. The pain, which by now had coloured the hand purple with restriction, became of secondary concern. It couldn't be ignored, yet I also knew that it couldn't be allowed to become a source of equally constrictive thought. Simply keeping quiet had never made so much sense or been quite so life-givingly important. It genuinely felt that my very life indeed depended on it.

And therein lies the beauty of it all – that the only thing which ever makes any real sense is the nameless presence of quiet itself. It's just that it often seems to take extreme circumstances or situations of great intensity to truly point us in its unlooked-for direction. One minute or so of breathing, of watching rather than grabbing all that mass of thought, brought a renewed feeling of deter- mination. The shivering subsided. I felt calm, clear and focused. I wanted out.

The Buddha is often quoted as having said that all

suffering comes from desire, from a wish to have things differently from how they appear to be. At that moment in time, if the desire to escape entailed sufferance further down the line, then a beast within was ready to rip its hands off and accept whatever may come.

Buoyed by such a steely refusal to accept that there wasn't some solution to the situation, my eyes fell for the first time on the topmost metal bar, the one whose movement as the roof slipped untied to the floor now had me trapped and unable to move. This was the one that was pressing down on top of the forearm, exerting enormous pressure on that part of the limb. The pain was becoming inspirational, a potential source of raw power that could work wonders if harnessed correctly. Every gram of strength that I had left to summon was directed toward lifting the iron tube.

Through sheer instinct, I suppose, I knew that I wouldn't have enough power to pull the bar far enough down to release my arm, but if I could only wrap the leg around it, it might just be enough. On the first attempt, the bar lifted up several centimetres. The wave of relief that flooded the entire arm remains indescribable, but I simply didn't have the strength to raise it enough to escape. As it thudded back down onto the arm, I suddenly remembered a film I'd seen years before, about a climber whose arm had become trapped between rocks in a truly remote part of south-western USA. *127 Hours*, as the film is called, recounts how the climber in question took the almighty decision to sever his own arm in order to escape.

I'm not in any way comparing the situation I was in

to the climber's ordeal, which lasted for six days, but the thought surfaced that I might have to resort to a similar course of action if I couldn't liberate my own crushed arm.

The cold was really starting to get to me by now. I'd been trapped for nearly 40 minutes, and the mixture of pines and beech that surround the glade were blocking all that remained of the sunlight. It was only about 2:30 in the afternoon, but the depth of the valley, and the way that it faced almost due north, meant that the shadows would continue to lengthen until all trace of the day was gone.

Every time I managed to summon the strength to lift the bar enough to give hope of escape, back down it came, crushing such indulgent thoughts beneath its cold metal. I was also becoming incredibly tired. Shivering and shaking, sweating yet frozen to the bone, I began, perhaps for the first time, to think that I might be beyond the reach of help. Everything I had tried so far had failed. The hand and fingers were becoming unresponsive and any attempt to massage life back into them only resulted in the confirmation that they were slowly losing all feeling.

The Casta continued to stare at me as placidly as only they can. I could look for no comfort in their shining eyes and, for once, no support either. For a moment, I thought I was totally and utterly alone and, even more than that, that nothing else existed outside of the scene I found myself in. For a second or two, I became a witness to my own personal nightmare, watching as if from some distant and detached platform. Rather than feeling trapped myself, I observed someone who was simply part of the scenery. And his struggles to escape were neither here nor there.

Maybe it was this change in perspective that gave me the strength to continue looking for a way out? I returned to the struggle, knowing that I just had to keep trying until I could try no more. It was then that my attention came to rest on the tattered blue safety rope dangling down from the roof of the feeder. I thought that if only I could tie a piece of it round the end of the topmost bar, that might give me enough leverage to release the arm at last.

I seized the opportunity with as much vigour as I could muster. Of course, the penknife with which I wanted to cut through the rope was dropped repeatedly into the thick layer of mud that surrounded me.

When I eventually managed to cut through the rope, the first attempt to attach it to the bar ended in failure. The only way to tie it firmly to the bar was to pass it through a hole at the end of the tube and secure it with a strong knot. God only knows how I tried to thread that muck-encrusted frayed excuse of a lifeline through that hole. It was simply too thick. When it was obvious that this wasn't going to provide me with a way out, I began rummaging through my coat pocket, the fingers of my right hand desperately searching for something to which the rope could be attached.

Call it what you will – luck, destiny, divine intervention – the fact of the matter is that out from the depths of that crumpled pocket came a split pin or R pin – a metal fastener that is used to secure and hold a bolt in place. They are incredibly useful little things having many uses, especially on the tractor.

As it was retrieved from the coat, I experienced a sudden sharp intake of breath. For the very first time since becoming trapped, something inside me saw the possibility of escape. There was nothing hopeful about it, neither was it born of desperation. I would say that it emerged from an almost cold sense of clarity, and ice-like certainty that here was the very thing that I hadn't known I'd been looking for.

Within seconds, I thrust it through the hole in the end of the bar and again to try to attach the rope. Even with a much greater width to poke the rope through, it wasn't until my fingers were beginning to cramp with the effort that I felt all was securely tied. Assuming the freestyle yoga position again, I wrapped a leg around the bar while at the same time pulling on its end with my right hand. As the roof lifted centimetre by centimetre, I grabbed hold of the rope and pulled with all my might. Just as it seemed that salvation was near, the pin popped out of the hole and down came the roof once more.

Without wasting a second on thought or even to take a breath, the pin was then re-threaded back through the hole but this time from the opposite direction. This meant that when I pulled down on the rope, the pressure would keep the pin firmly attached to the bar. On the second attempt and within seconds of manoeuvring myself into position, the extra purchase that the rope now afforded me meant that the roof sprung up the desired number of centimetres for me to be able to yank out what by now had become a quite badly crushed arm.

The dull aching pain that immediately engulfed the entire limb did away with any celebratory sigh of relief or grateful scream of deliverance. I gathered my coat and assorted things together, climbed back on to the tractor and dropped the bale of hay into the feeder. That done, I headed back down the track to the old barn where the Galloways were housed for winter. Instinct told me that I had to leave a bale of hay next to their pen, because I wasn't going to be around for a while.

The clarity that such pain or trauma brings can be laser-like at times. The sheer magnitude of the suffering stops thinking dead in its tracks and in the ensuing quietness what comes is crystal clear. It was obvious that an ambulance was needed but still the cows had to come first. Corky, suicide, cows, healing. They had to come first.

Having dropped the bale off I headed up the lane to the house. By now, in its own quiet way, the pain had become immense. Diana greeted me at the and door and, having shown her the crumpled excuse of an arm, I asked her to phone for an ambulance. The journey to the hospital in Carcassonne took around one hour and I am sure every single second of it was etched into the grimacing frown that had set up camp upon my forehead.

Once inside the hospital building, I was very quickly assessed and moved into a side room. Within minutes a surgeon had come to look at the arm. Without beating around the bush, he told me very directly that the arm required immediate surgery if there was to be any chance of saving not only the hand itself but its future mobility.

I was swiftly undressed by the nurses in attendance and whisked off to the operating theatre. The pain in combination with the urgency of the situation meant that there was very little time to think about what appeared to be happening. I experienced no fear or trepidation concerning what might be ahead. There was only what can be described as a surrender to whatever Life had in store.

Before the anaesthetist sent me sliding down into oblivion, there were a few moments in which I reflected on this apparent lack of fear. I remembered that as a child, there had been some difficulties with the anaesthetic following a minor operation. It's said that I showed a reluctance to return to the land of the living, which had given a certain amount of cause for concern.

Since then and increasingly so as I had got older, there had been a subtle background anxiety regarding the thought of having another general anaesthetic. It was with some surprise, therefore, that I observed myself in total acceptance of the whole situation. Even the vast array of piercingly bright lights that lit up the operating theatre did little to disturb the mindful bubble into which I seemed to have slid. I suppose that in some simplistic way, I just wanted the pain to end and surrender to this silenced any thoughts of fear.

I woke up several hours later in a private room and was immediately aware of an absence of any pain. What a blessed relief to feel free of that incessant pounding.

# Epilogue

The anaesthetic of course was still coursing through the veins and whatever I was hooked up to via the drip was helping to maintain the sense of deep relaxation.

When, a day later, the surgeon unravelled the bandages and invited me to look at his handiwork, the full impact of the severity of the accident really hit me for the first time. I've never had the opportunity to actually look inside my arm before, nor anyone else's come to think of it. I'll skip the finer, more graphic, details but yes, I was left under no illusion whatsoever as to the extent of the injury.

At the very limit of my French, I understood that I would be operated on again in two days' time, to further relieve the pressure and to remove sections of muscle that had died as a direct result of the prolonged crushing of the arm. It was in between these two trips to the theatre that the Ramana-inspired self-enquiry really began in earnest. The questioning of every single thought became an automatic action, a routine investigation into the very source of all mental activity. I can only say that it was a most natural response to a situation in which thoughts could run gloriously amok if given free rein to do so.

'There but for the grace of God go I. There but for the grace of God go I,' sandwiched between 'To whom does this thought occur?' Never before had I practised such enquiry with the level of determination that I discovered during those days. I could feel the thoughts welling up, tumbling over and over like a river in full spate but never being allowed to take root. The questioning of their origin instantly nipped them in the bud and this permitted an almost total acceptance of everything that was happening.

The third operation, a week or more later, involved closing the wound as much as possible and grafting a piece of skin from the left thigh to a part of the arm where skin had been previously removed by the surgeon.

The four days that followed, being confined to bed without permission to get up, were probably the toughest of all. It seemed during that period that all the thoughts in the entire universe had gathered their forces for a determined assault on my somewhat fragile defences. This was particularly so at night when the hourly visits from nurses, carers and other personnel slowed right down to a trickle. 'Infection!' they shouted. 'You hand-icapped cripple,' and other such nagging statements. During one especially challenging night, when a bout of flu first reared its feverish head, I remembered having read that Ramana had encouraged devotees to lay such bombardments at the feet of The Lord. 'Give all away' he had said, guiding those with ears to hear towards a non-identification with all mental activity. Recall of such dear advice really carved right through that sticky and genuinely sickly web of thought and in the quietness that followed, I knew I would be able to leave hospital within a week.

The first few days back home passed by in a blur of tiredness and happy reunion. To be back with the kids, to ruffle their hair and cuddle up on the sofa was wonderful beyond belief. Diana, who had looked after me so tirelessly during the month of hospitalisation, was able to relax a

Epilogue

little and it was so good to see her face become less
harried and fraught with concern.

Mum and Dad were still at the farm, having flown out
straight after the accident. Feeding the dogs, filling the
log basket and keeping the house in good order were
their way of saying welcome home Dave. With such
support, I was able to make the transition from quiet
hospital bed to full-on family life as smoothly as possible.

Seeing the cows for the first time in weeks resulted in
a strange mixture of elation and frustration. I was so very
happy to see them, to smell their sweet breath and look
into those inky eyes again. However, I also realised that
I couldn't just get in among them as would have been
the case before, for fear of injuring the arm still further.
It was a sobering moment and one which brought feelings
of both motivation *and* disheartenment.

One of Gabi and Elie's favourite bedtime stories is *The
Hare and the Tortoise*. I can't remember how many times
we've read it together, but it's become a firm favourite
of mine too. The words with which the fable is brought
to a close have become a constant source of inspiration:
'Slow and steady wins the race'. As much as I may have
wanted to, I couldn't suddenly magic my arm back into
its previous range of mobility or do the hundred and one
things that needed doing every day on the farm in ways
that I had been used to. It's not about that anyway. The
outer only exists to bring one to the point of total
surrender. Like a plant that gradually weaves its way
through layers of stone and tarmac, there exists an insistent
force that fans the flames of determination. Yes, I was

determined to recover as much use of the injured limb as possible but this in itself is only a faint echo of the resolve that desires nothing less than self-illumination. Slow and steady wins the race.

In the weeks and months that followed my return home and with the support of an incredibly forceful physiotherapist, there was a dramatic improvement in both the strength and flexibility of the hand and arm. And it seemed to be part of the whole package that the physio just happened to be completely blind. It appeared to me each time that I saw him that he had learned to see through his fingers. His touch, feather-like and torturous in equal measure looked right down into those places where the muscles or tendons remained tight and tied-up by the trauma. He laughed the most each time I howled with pain. '*Trop cher*' he shouted if I didn't meet his challenge head on. At times it felt utterly brutal, more painful even than the accident itself, yet the opportunities that the sessions and exercises presented for putting determination, discipline and stubborn insistence into practice were priceless beyond measure.

And, in the midst of the most painful sessions of all, somehow woven into the fabric of the torture itself, there were moments of pure and unbridled comedy. One of the treatments involved placing several small glass containers onto the affected forearm. These seemingly innocent little cups were connected to a machine via tubes, which created a suction effect wherever they were placed on the skin. The technique is officially known as Cupping Therapy.

As Cyrille, the physio, explained, it was necessary to separate the skin from the muscle, fused as they had become under the prolonged crushing weight of the iron tubes during the accident. He took several minutes to elaborate on the method, assuring me that it would swiftly return the skin to its former state of elasticity.

As the cups were being prepared, Cyrille began, once again, to laugh. He even hummed a little tune, then warbled away in his heavily accented English. Music was an ever-present feature of his *cabinet*. His playlists were a wonderful mix of anything from hip-hop to Beethoven's fifth symphony. Within seconds of turning the machine on, however, all appreciation of whatever was wafting into to the room through the speakers instantly evaporated. PAIN! Unbelievable levels of beyond-excruciating pain. Never before or since have I experienced such depths of physical unbearableness. For several moments, it genuinely felt as if the arm was being flayed alive, and as I peeped between my scrunched-up eyelids, the blood that was trickling from the reopened wounds meant that it quite possibly was!

We can talk about pain thresholds as long as we like but that was something else. At the peak of the ordeal, when it felt that any reasonable limit had been passed several agonising minutes before, I became aware once again of the background presence of the music. I recognised the song immediately – 'What is Love?' – a club-classic from the early 90s. Without thought or awareness of what was to come, I suddenly found myself caught up in the undeniably catchy chorus and turning to meet Cyrille head-on, screeched out through clenched teeth, 'Baby don't hurt me.'

It took a few seconds for the words to take effect. At first, the *kiné's* response was nothing more than some sort of snort. His eyes flickered, staring out unseeing into the world and then he began to laugh. Great thunderous peals of laughter from such a big man filled the entire room and thankfully brought the session to an end. Comedy!

And now, at the time of writing, I'm happy to say that the arm and hand have made an almost complete recovery. Even the thumb, which the surgeon said would remain but a useless onlooker for the rest of my earthly life, has regained all of its previous movement and dexterity. Yes, there is an impressive scar running the full length of the forearm and the graft of skin, taken from the inner thigh to close an uncloseable gap, has been named 'the chicken wing' by the kids, resembling as it does the uncooked version of the above-mentioned portion. They are happy, too, that Papa can do all the things with them that at one point might never have seemed possible again, particularly their own chaotic, rough-and-tumble version of no-holds-barred wrestling.

The key to such a happy state of affairs, well, farm work really. The hours of physio helped, of course, quite wonderfully so, yet the day to day running of the farm has been crucial. It calls for such a varied and wide-ranging use of the arm and hand, anything from the heavy stuff like felling old dead trees for firewood to the finer work of screwing nuts onto bolts and so on. Life brought its crushing weight to bear on the arm and Life has provided the means for such swift and straightforward healing. Of course there were moments of raw frustration, especially early on, but this constant demand on the injured area has forced it to remember how to work and how very well it has done.

I can be with the cows again without any fear whatsoever of further damaging the arm and for this I am eternally grateful. Just seeing them is often enough, and physical contact isn't always necessary, yet getting right in there among them is where the magic really lies. And I can't deny that they too have changed somehow during this whole period. They are definitely softer, somehow, especially the Casta, and less prone to sudden movements in my presence. Pellie for example, the great gentle giant of a Casta ox, has now and again got his great-horned head stuck behind the feeding barriers. He has learned to manoeuvre his way in, but on occasion is at a loss to get himself out. While waiting for me to liberate him, he is calm and quiet and collected. There is not a flicker of panic nor a single second of fear in his shining eyes. His strength is immense. He weighs at least a ton yet stands there as quiet as a lamb, letting me guide his magnificent horns back out through the bars. Our lives have become so entwined and interconnected, that whatever affects me affects them too, and vice versa. I would not have it any other way.

The re-education of the arm has merely been the way in, the further opening of a door that leads one stoically back to one's Self, to the home that was never actually left in the first place.

There are no accidents, only milestones and signposts. Such are the workings of love.

# The Cows

We currently have the privilege of sharing our farm with thirty-five cows – 24 Casta and 11 Galloways. There are bulls young and old, oxen, adult mothers and a veritable gaggle of teenage heifers. The calves are the obvious pride and joy of each herd, indulged in and spoilt rotten by their doting mothers.

To enter into their world, to really come close and in some way surrender to their own cloven-hooved rhythm is to discover a plethora of diverse and fascinating strands. So many elements, so rich and unspeakably varied are woven together into a single seamless whole. Unpicking the threads that combine to create such a living tapestry gives a glimpse into the heart of the Being with Cows project, particularly from a grounded, practical perspective.

## NATURAL FARMING

We raise the cows organically and in the most natural way possible. Their diet consists only of what the landscape provides on a seasonal basis. In winter, when opportunities to browse and graze are more scarce, they eat organic hay and alfalfa, sourced from within 20 kilometres of the farm.

Why organic? Well, because first and foremost the natural world is deserving of our utmost respect, care and stewardship. Assuming the role of guardians of such a precious, well-preserved haven as Raulet is both a great responsibility and a source of inspiration.

The wellbeing of all the inhabitants of the 100 hectares is as important to us as that of the cows themselves. Being pesticide and chemical-free is the first basic step to ensuring that not only is our earthly footprint very light, but that everything from orchids to oaks and the ever-fascinating praying mantis is given the opportunity to thrive.

Leaving large areas of the woodland untouched, where brambles can creep and crawl across the landscape and the skeletons of fallen trees bring heaven to earth for a mass of mushrooms and mini-beasts, is our way of saying thank you.

Watching wild boar grunt their grumpy way through the woods, snorting and snuffling as they go, brings confirmation that it is simply the right thing to do. Such thickets of impenetrable thorn are a sanctuary of sorts for these magnificently wild ones, hunted as they are from August right through to March.

Perhaps it's the insects in particular who indicate the necessity to be kind and caring to the earth. Standing in any of the meadows at Raulet in the full flush of summer, one cannot fail to be moved by the sheer isness of the sound that greets the ears. A wholesome mass of crickets, grass-hoppers and hardy cicadas chirping their hearts out. It is, without doubt, a most humbling experience, a sound-bath of such natural intensity. It invigorates, revitalises and invites the listener to just forget themselves, if but only for a few extraordinary moments.

In certain meadows not far from the farm, where the idea of improvement has stolen and spirited away such natural wealth, that signature sound of summer is deafening in its absence. Of course our long-legged friends are still there, but in achingly far fewer numbers. There is a sadness in such silence.

Apart from in winter, the cows feed from an incredibly rich range of grasses, herbs, wildflowers, leaves, nuts and even fungi. This is the beauty of raising such ancient and rustic breeds – they retain the knowledge of how to stay well eating only what nature itself provides.

This also applies to their instinctive understanding of selecting certain plants, leaves, or berries according to their medicinal properties. Nursing mothers for example will seek out stinging nettles as a source of replenishment, rich as they are in amino acids, protein, flavonoids, and bone-building minerals like iron, calcium, magnesium, potassium, and zinc. It's an instinctual action that serves both them and the little one they are nourishing.

In autumn, they will gorge themselves on acorns and chestnuts that lie scattered over acres of forest floor. It's often the case, especially as night falls, that this hoovering up of the woodland's bounty is done in the company of the wild boar and deer who also call the farm their home.

It brings a sense of wild, mysterious joy to see the cows in the midst of their undomesticated neighbours and with the Casta in particular. I've often felt that there's not really anything that stands between them except for their unsightly ear tags.

The landscape at Raulet is a beautiful upland patchwork of meadow and deciduous woodland. Deep ravines carve through the flanks of some of the eastern-most hillsides and its highest point, 730 metres above sea level, affords the most glorious view of the Pyrenees. The Casta and Galloways have access to every meadow, hillside and hidden dell. They know it all and return over and over again to favourite places, shady spots that blot out the summer sun or hollows that protect from buffeting winter winds.

They have carved endless paths through the woods in the short time that we have been at Raulet. Brambles brushed aside, old branches broken and trampled into the forest floor contribute in many ways to the wellbeing of each patch that they browse their way through. Whilst Being with Cows doesn't officially consider itself to be a rewilding project per se, the cows have an incredibly beneficial effect on each habitat type that they encounter. There is no need whatsoever to create detailed, office-designed management plans – just let them get in there and do their thing. They know what to do and I trust them implicitly, just as I trust nature to provide all that they ever should need.

The Galloways in particular can be considered to be quite fantastic managers of all types of terrain, so unfussy are they in their approach to filling their bellies. From the roughest of field margins to scrub, and the tender leaves of young emerging saplings in spring, they help to keep things in some kind of balance.

When we first moved to the farm, large areas of land had been left to go its own way for many years. Nature's desire to return all to woodland had led many acres, especially the meadows, to become smothered under the scratchy sprawl of countless brambles and blackthorn. Whilst this provides excellent cover for a whole range of birds and animals, it was clear that it had meant the loss of thousands of nectar-rich wildflowers.

In their constant search for nourishment, the cows have opened up great swathes of these colonised meadows, carving a way through stands of brush and bracken. And in their wake, little by little, the colour has returned in such beautiful splashes of yellow and violet and rose. The clover, the orchids, trefoil, bedstraw and mint that have sprung up along these trails offer rich-pickings for the winged insects that rely on such provision for their survival. Belly-led movement that benefits the bees is but one example of the way in which the cows can bring balance back into a landscape. That they are part of something that leads to a most inspiring all-inclusivity is simply wonderful, satisfied customers on every corner.

Both breeds, especially the Casta, have largely escaped the intensive selection process that has seen many more populous breeds reduced to a mere ghost of their former, original selves. I admit that there may be more than a hint of my own stuff projected onto them but the way they retain a barely concealable sense of something raw and elemental is at times quite inspirational.

Take July for example, one of our Galloway mothers. There is no other way to say it but that she just looks so old, ancient in fact, something untouched by modernity or even the passage of time. She's only eight, not even middle-aged yet, but that face speaks of things before the world itself was born.

And the horns of the Casta, carried with dignified ease, are great indicators of their unbroken ancientness. Often lyre-shaped, always so gracefully curved in one way or another, they reach out into the world around them. They are mightily impressive works of art. Dangerous of course and always to be respected. Weapons of defence or attack surely, but so very much more. I'm convinced that the horns are antennae of sorts, receivers and transmitters of great significance. In sunshine, rain, sleet and snow, they pierce the air itself, tapping into a source of essential background information. Through them, air meets the earth and the cow rests in between.

In many ways they represent a cow's individuality, as unique as our own fingerprints. They are sense organs which have a stream of blood coursing through them and are connected to the sinus system, allowing air to circulate through the bone. They make a subtle but important contribution to the wellbeing of the cow and to the quality of her digestion and metabolism.

Shining horns represent a healthy and happy cow and in happy cows, with ample room to move, those weapons become instruments of play. Locking horns doesn't always have to mean violent struggle.

## CATHARS

As well as being so richly endowed with such a wealth of natural heritage, the wider landscape surrounding the farm is equally celebrated for its fascinating cultural history, none more so than that of the Cathars.

The Cathars were a religious group who flourished in south-western France towards the end of the 12th century. The movement took root in an area often referred to as the Languedoc, broadly bordered by the Mediterranean Sea, the Pyrenees, and the rivers Garonne, Tarn and Rhône, corresponding to the new French region of Occitanie (or the old French regions of Languedoc-Roussillon and Midi-Pyrenees).

Their rejection of the corruptive practices that in their eyes were becoming increasingly prevalent in the Roman

Catholic Church of the time led, ultimately, to their complete and utter destruction.

Their ultimate goal was to obtain purity in this earthly life, which they saw everywhere corrupted by the devil.

The head of the Catholic Church, Pope Innocent III, called a formal Crusade against the Cathars of the Languedoc region and appointed a series of military leaders to head his Holy Army.

From 1208, a war of terror was waged against the indigenous population of the Languedoc and their rulers, many of whom, if not already converted, were sympathetic to the Cathar movement and all it stood for. In modern terms, it was nothing short of genocide. Within a few years the first papal Inquisition, manned by the Dominican Order of monks, was established explicitly to wipe out the last remnants of resistance. The Languedoc started its long economic decline from one of the richest regions of Europe to become the poorest region in France; and the language of the area, Occitan began its descent from the foremost literary language in Europe to a regional dialect.

Our farm and nearest village of Saint-Benoît lie right in the heart of what was once Cathar country. The whole landscape is littered with the ruins of Cathar châteaux, from Peyrepertuse to Termes and the iconic Montségur.

All very interesting and historic, but what of the cows? Well, if the Casta and their ancestors are truly as ancient as they are reputed to be, then it is perhaps more than a mere flight of fancy to entertain the idea that certain members of the breed bore witness to the whole movement, from beginning to bloody end.

Their character certainly reflects the ancient history of the whole region, a land once so beloved by its Occitan-speaking inhabitants. They are fiercely independent and have also been subjected to attempts to wipe them from the face of the earth. In the 1950s and 1960s, the Casta, like so many 'non-efficient' local breeds, had to contend with a governmental policy that wished to pressure them into extinction. Reproduction was officially discouraged, with the focus falling on breeds considered to be more productive and capable of supporting the desire to be nationally self-sufficient in food-stuffs.

Unlike the Cathars, however, the Casta have endured. The 'Devil's Cow' as it was once called plods on, a living link with the torturous past of this magnificent land. They carry the memory, however deeply buried, of all that has come to pass in these foothills and mountains. One look in their eyes will tell you they remember.

That they are still here, albeit so thinly scattered across the land, is testament in some way to their deep allegiance to stubbornness. *Têtu* from nose to tail-tip, they simply don't give in. Perhaps the spirit of the Cathars lives on in their oft-maligned form. They are of the same earth after all.

## KIDS AND COWS AND CALVES

Elie has an affection for all the cows at Raulet but particularly so for Petou, the enormous Casta ox. Theirs is a special relationship, one founded on total trust. It is very much a little and large situation, Elie being dwarfed by the sheer bulk of his splendidly horned friend. They are so tender with each other, sharing long moments of such gentle togetherness that this beaming onlooker is moved to the very depths of his heart.

At times, when the sight of their bonding becomes almost too perfect to bear, there comes the sense that such scenes represent the absolute flowering of the whole project. For a little while, innocence reigns supreme. It is Garden of Eden stuff.

While these outpourings of brotherly love are present whenever the two are together, there have been countless other occasions when both Gabi, Elie and at times some of their friends have had heart-warming contact with the cows.

Bottle feeding young calves is always an opportunity for coming in close and is something that Gabi usually takes very seriously. Firm but patient in equal measure, he instinctively understands the importance of letting the little one feed in total calm.

Fortunately, it is very rare that we have to resort to such things, having such wonderfully caring mothers, yet every time that the need has arisen, Gabi has stepped up to the plate. Happy when the bottle is emptied, concerned when the calf can't latch on, he has something of the mother hen about him that makes caring for waifs and strays an automatic response to finding a young one in need.

The youngsters amongst the Casta and Galloways are often irresistibly drawn to any children they encounter. On one occasion, this inquisitiveness became something akin to a thinly disguised love-in. It was high up on the flanks of one of the hillside meadows. The unseasonably hot June day had sweated its way into a most pleasantly mellow evening. With Diana away from the farm, Gabi, Elie and I went walkabout on the land and our footsteps eventually led us to the Casta.

Profiting from the drop in temperature that usually comes with the close of day at this altitude, the Casta were busy grazing when we found them. Sitting down to watch, we were immediately approached by several of the youngest heifers. It was their first spring and they looked in fantastic condition. For several moments, they jostled for position, nudging each other ever closer to where we were sitting. After a brief period in which both the boys and the love-lies seemed to be quietly communing, Reine and then Rishi stepped forward to make their acquaintance.

What ensued was quite wonderful to behold, a meeting founded on youthful innocence and trust. The heifers came and went, then came back again, unable to curb a curiosity that for some of their breed is something to be acknowledged but not acted upon. That the two sides had apparently thrown off any sense of fear or reservation was the greatest cause for celebration.

They were simply together for a while, united by their youth and unthinking acceptance of each other's company.

When we parted, the boys and myself were escorted to the fence by this troop of teenagers, unwilling perhaps to bring the party to a close. It was Friday night after all.

## COWS AS SENTIENT BEINGS

Reine came to live with us in 2016, a wizened old Casta grandmother. She was impeccably dignified, a noble woman to whom good manners and grace came so effortlessly. Unlike her younger namesake, she carried an air of seen-it-all-before acceptance. One look in her eyes would confirm that here was one who simply *understood*, a living, breathing fount of peace and saintly wisdom.

She came to us as a gift, included in the purchase of four Casta heifers. It was suggested that her presence would help smooth their relocation from one farm and herd to another and so it proved to be.

By this stage in her life, the march of time was already evident in her body. She had reached the grand old age of 19 and had become a little unsteady on her legs. That she had lived so long and well after a difficult start to life was testament to both her own will to endure and the love and care that was heaped upon her by the farmer who had previously looked after her.

# The Cows

He bought her from a small farm in the mountains, where an almost peasant-like existence continued. She had been confined in an old stone barn almost from birth, stuck in the shadows of the farmer's allegiance to the old ways. Wim, the man life sent to spring her from what was little more than a medieval prison cell, said that when he collected her, she was virtually blind from living in the darkness. What's more, her hooves were so long that they looked like Turkish slippers, curling up and over at the front end.

This made walking a difficult and painful exercise, unused as she was to having the freedom to walk upon field or forest floor. What a blessing for them both that her escape became. Wim, devoted to nursing her back to health, both inside and out, found a soulmate of sorts and Reine of course was finally free to put footsteps on the earth.

By the time she came to us, the often intense dynamics of herd-life for the Casta, largely passed her by. No longer a queen or able to bring new life into the world, hers was a happy and well-earned retirement. Although mostly left to her own devices by the rest of the tribe, this elder woman was still at times a respected and looked-to member, a source of calm and reassurance when the need arose.

One of the best meadows we had when we lived at Mirepoix, was a mile or so down the road. The most obvious and practical way of getting the cows there to graze was to walk them down said lane. It was always an occasion that brought both delight and a background sense of tension. The possibility of things getting out of hand was always present, unfenced as most of the roadside was.

Usually, all was well. I can only remember one incident that led to short-term mayhem, when a lone cyclist got somehow enmeshed in the midst of the excited Galloways. I only ever moved the cows to that meadow on a Sunday morning, as early as possible before people were up and about in their cars.

That particular day, the lycra-clad *cycliste* had refused our polite request to wait but a minute before the cows were on their way. He insisted, equally politely, that he would continue. Within moments of climbing back on his bike, he was engulfed by a heaving mass of Galloways, few in number but buzzing at the prospect of the grazing to come. In a vain attempt to outrun them, he pedalled faster and faster, yet this only served to add fuel to their fire. I suppose it was nerves that got to him in the end, for, unwilling to accept the sudden appearance of this strange and unlooked for *peloton*, he resorted to screaming at them.

Isi, an excitable but generally good-humoured mother, decided that the fields bordering the road were probably a better place to be. It's all for one and one for all with the Galloways and as she broke through the single-stringed excuse of a temporary fence, the rest followed quickly in her wake.

She hadn't liked being shouted at any more than most people. Cows feel things so very deeply. Sensitive to the core, her flight reflected a natural love of harmony, of peaceful calm in which the important work of eating and sleeping can carry on unhindered.

Reine's ability to guide the Casta down the same road, when their initial uncertainty kept them back from the open gateway, was but another example of their innate sensitivity. Ignored at almost all other times, it was she who would always break that invisible barrier, crossing from meadow to lane without panic or undue fuss. When she had delivered the herd to their fresh grazing, she disappeared once more into the background. What an unassuming star!

When she passed away at the age of 22, I genuinely felt as if I'd lost a lifelong friend. She spent her last few weeks with the Galloways, the flat meadow where they overwintered being kinder on her unstable legs than the sloping land where her fellow Casta were. The Galloways had accepted her without too much fuss. Yes, they were boisterous in the initial act of greeting, yet quickly took her into the fold and left her pretty much alone.

Her death, however, when it came, triggered an outpouring of emotion that I had never before witnessed in the cows. On discovery of her body, already devoid of breath or any warmth, Leith the bull firstly sniffed her all over and then launched into the most moving of throaty roars. It filled the entire valley with a deep sense of longing, a lament perhaps that certainly brought tears to my eyes.

The rest of the herd were also highly animated, returning again and again to sniff and nudge and bellow. Can there truly be any doubt that these beautiful beings are as subject to the same tides of feeling and emotion as we are? It's absolute nonsense to think otherwise.

When Olivia, the first Casta calf to be born on the farm, made her appearance, her instantly besotted mother Llivia was so beside herself with joy that she too shook the valley with such undiluted sound. Her lowing, unforgettably deep and lasting, alerted her herd-mates to the fact that something of the momentous was unfolding, that there, in her corner of the field, her whole life had suddenly changed forever.

Long will it live in the memory, that scene of unbridled celebration. Every member of the clan, thrilled beyond measure, came to pay homage and respect to that glistening bundle of love. For her papa, Mascarde, it was his first experience of fatherhood. He sniffed and snorted and danced, cavorting and calling out to all the world that here lay his firstborn, the fruit of autumnal labours. That Gabi was with me to witness those priceless scenes made everything all the more perfect. 'Well boy,' I shouted to Mascarde, 'That's you and me then.' I swear he looked at me with an extra twinkle in his eye, confirming a shared belonging to some fatherly brotherhood.

The rest of the mothers-to-be, all carrying more of Mascarde's seed, were fascinated by Olivia's arrival. For a moment, it seemed that Llivia herself was in danger of being swamped by a wave of maternal longing, but instinct is a powerful thing and she stood her ground, even pushing back those who ranked higher than her in the hierarchy.

And these are but the briefest examples, fleeting glimpses into a world that is mostly hidden from public view. Everything we value as human beings, from compassion to kindness and unfathomable love, is fully present in the cows. Jealousy too, cruelty at times and pain. We share so very much and our differences are really so few. Cowfulness! Watch this space.

## VOLUNTEERS

Since beginning the journey with the cows in 2015, we have hosted more than eighty volunteers from all over the world. Connecting via HelpX, WWOOF and Workaway, helpers have come on work exchange, becoming part of the family for weeks or months at a time. Their support has been invaluable.

Fencing, tree planting, cutting firewood, green gardening . . . the list goes on and on. Without heavy machinery, it's not so easy to manage large tracts of land that is constantly trying its best to return to scrub or woodland. Perhaps rewilding is the solution, just letting it all go exactly as it pleases!

Without such willing and often happy hands, it's quite possible that all attempts to at the very least keep meadows and forest paths open, would have slowly been swallowed by those decidedly unbeatable brambles. One hundred hilly hectares against one man and his strimmer hardly seems much of a fair contest at all!

Some have been more naturally aligned with the cows than others, tumbling head over heels upon first contact.

Elias arrived in the midst of the driest, hottest summer in recorded history. An apprentice stonemason from Germany, I immediately warmed to his deep quietness and incredibly dry sense of humour. For long periods of time, we rarely spoke. Where is the need when words only serve to block a steady undercurrent of peace? He was conscientious in everything he did, working efficiently and with great concentration.

What endeared him to me more than anything else was the absolute kindness he expressed in contact with all the animals at Raulet. From our dogs Bramble, Beith and Mila, Couscous the cat and Pingu the physically challenged hen, to every single one of the cows, his respectful, quiet approach has granted him access to their trust and acceptance.

All that is except for Paula the rebellious Galloway. Their first meeting ended with her invitation that he should leave the field with immediate effect. What a glorious scene for those who appreciate a healthy slice of the absurd with their daily bread and butter. Please picture, if for but a moment, the most idyllic of country meadows. Wildflowers, bushes and ancient trees standing guard along the margins. A gentle breeze to temper the heat of yet another scorchingly hot day. Fat, contented Galloways, cud-chewing their way into heaven.

Enter Elias, a young man at the height of his physical power, tall, athletic and exuding an air of all-round wellbeing.

# The Cows

There is one Galloway who sits apart from the rest. Even in the summer heat she has retained her shaggy-black coat, giving her more than a hint of wilderness. She acknowledges the sudden arrival of this stranger, scanning him with her unreadable eyes.

I hold my tongue as he approaches, fascinated by what might unfold. He knows nothing of her character, her dedication to unpredictability. When only a handful of metres lie between them, she rises, stretches along the length of her spine and attacks. Head-down, tail up, she covers the gap in seconds flat.

It's not a *real* charge so to speak, nothing of the life-threatening kind. She simply wants him out of the way. Long will it live in the memory, that image of a role-reversed David and Goliath. Elias reaches out a long arm to touch her face, an attempt to make space between them. Uh-oh!

How carefully he reversed his way across that meadow. How stubbornly she ignored all calls to desist. What a baptism of fire for one who came to love the cows unreservedly, all of them.

Upon returning to Raulet a year later, Elias had opportunities to deepen his relationship with the cows with one episode in particular bringing me to call him The Ascended One. Being back home in Worcestershire is always a delight, difficult as it is to leave the farm for any length of time. We had been back for several days when I got a message from Elias that Orion, our beloved Galloway bullock, had developed quite a problem in one of his eyes. It had closed, was all puffed up and seemed to be attracting a host of persistent flies. Pink eye is its name and whatever its cause, from bacteria to dust or spiky thorns, it can lead to great suffering and even blindness.

As always, unless the situation calls for immediate intervention from the vet, I prefer to try to find a natural solution before resorting to antibiotics and so on. Elias was onboard with this right from the start and to his great and everlasting credit, he sought out Orion every single day until our return. What made this act of compassion even more impressive was that the Galloways at that time had the run of a large patch of forest, open in places but thicket-like and bramble-covered in others.

At least twice a day, often in stifling heat, he went to Orion and gently bathed his eye with a herbal infusion that included ricin oil. Ably assisted by Aurelie, a friend who had set up camp in one of the older buildings on the farm, Orion was also treated to bucketfuls of camomile tea. All in the name of love.

Such a commitment to the care of those who had been left in his charge was what lifted Elias up, in my eyes, into the realm of Saints and Masters.

We remain in regular contact, The Ascended One and me.

And yes, even Paula came to be touched by his inherent goodness. Gone were the tantrums in his company. In came acceptance of his commitment to non-violence. Some trees are not to be toppled.

## CASTA

We have been raising Castas since the winter of 2015. When the first three heifers arrived, skittish and incredibly sensitive to their new environment, we knew virtually nothing about their precarious status, their history and truly iconic place in the folklore of the Central French Pyrenees.

All we knew was that this was reputedly a very ancient breed, who seemed to be a living link between the modern breeds so pummelled by insatiable market forces and the Auroch, the primeval, wild ancestor of all native cattle breeds still found in Europe today.

This presence of an almost wild depth of sensitivity, of an instinct not diluted by centuries of selective breeding (as has happened with many other breeds), has allowed us a very privileged glimpse into a world untroubled by thought and speculation. The Castas, by way of their natural transparency, are for us a spotless mirror, in which all of who we think we might be is bounced right back.

## Origins and History

It is said that the Casta breed originated in the Val d'Aran in northern Spain, at the sources of the Garonne river and are the result of the encounter between two types of Spanish and French cattle – those of the Iberian tribes in what is now the Central Spanish Pyrenees and the Celtic tribes who inhabited what is now the Central French Pyrenees.

Whatever its true origin, this iconic race of the Pyrenees is genuinely very ancient and is one of the first races cited in the history of the cattle breeds of the South of France. At the beginning of the twentieth century, it populated the high-altitude Pyrenees, from the Tarbaise region to Foix. In France today, it is traditionally recognised as originating from two distinct regions:

The valley of Aure in the Hautes-Pyrénées (type 'Aurois')

The basin of St-Girons and Couserans in Ariège (type 'St-Gironnais')

## Into Decline

By the early 1980s, the Casta breed faced a very real threat of extinction. In 1983, the number of females was down to a mere 76, spread between 12 different herds.

Their decline it seems was a side-effect of the general process of livestock specialisation, when economic, commercial, technical and administrative pressures began to influence which breeds farmers selected.

However, a small number of impassioned breeders acted to ensure the conservation of as many females as possible.

By 2010, despite the efforts of this small group of truly dedicated breeders and conservationists, the population of females had risen to just 208 individuals in 39 herds. By

2015, the population consisted of 336 females. The number of herds had increased to 52.

## Characteristics

The Castas are typically known for their incredible rusticity. They are regarded to be of a robust temperament, being both vigorous and energetic and, through centuries of exposure to the extremes of the mountainous climate in the Central Pyrenees, are what could be called a quite 'weather-resistant' breed! The rich milk produced by the incredibly maternal mothers gave rise to the manufacture of the celebrated Bethmale cheese. The oxen, alive and alert, were employed in wagons, or for the logging of wood in the mountains. Since 1986, the breed has been used in several nature reserves in France as a tool for the management of wetland habitats.

## Judith

One of the most grounded and approachable of them all. Trustworthy, caring and gentle in equal measure. A soulmate of sorts to whom I will ever rest in gratitude.

## Jacinthe

Sensitive to the extreme upon whom domestication sits as the thinnest disguise. Fiercely protective mother.

## Lys

Current queen and unmovable steady presence. Has mellowed with the passing of time and has now become both reliable and gentile.

## Llorelei
Physically speaking a very slender member of the herd, yet she has produced some of the most robust calves of any of the Casta mothers.

## Lotus
A name that speaks of serenity yet Lotus is very much the strong character, incredibly independent and often happy to mind her own business away from the rest of the group.

## Llivia
Shiny as can be inside and out. Always in great health and the most gentle and doting of mothers.

## Maluna
Among the adult females, she remains at the bottom of the pecking order, last to eat or drink.

## Rishi
Another kindred spirit, capable of such tender, loving contact. Above all else, quite simply a wonderful friend.

## Reine
Kind, calm and always curious, she carries a sense of gracefulness with such natural ease.

## Pellie
A golden-hearted giant of an ox who is nothing but an everlasting gentleman. Hates having to walk on tarmac, tip-toeing his massive way if asked to do so.

# The Cows

**Petou**

An equally impressive ox. Adores being scratched and stroked all over except for his head. Any attempt to do so activates his instant withdrawal from the scene.

**Qupe**

The youngest ox who was born blind and incredibly weak. Now, with full vision and several hundred kilos of pure muscle, he cuts a very fine figure of a young man.

**Ruth**

Self-assured and independent, this young lady is very sure of her place in the world.

**Sandi**

Such steadiness and self-confidence exudes from this teen-ager. Mature beyond her years perhaps and undisputed queen of the younger females.

**Sally**

Softness personified, incredibly inquisitive and a genuine pleasure to be around.

**Silvia**

A rough-coated punk whose almost invisible presence means she often feeds first when others of her age wait patiently at the back of the queue.

**Silvy**

Easily the furriest of the Casta with the most liquidly beautiful eyes. Approachable right from the start and now a most valued quiet presence on the farm.

**Grace**
Born in the depths of the forest, she retains an air of wildness and something of the elemental.

**Katie**
Always seeking the exit, ready to flee at the slightest sign of something amiss. This spirited young heifer will slowly ground and carry her Casta-ness with greater poise.

**Twig**
A shy boy who too was delivered amongst the trees. Timid by nature, he is slowly finding his feet and place in the midst of the herd.

**Billy**
Such soulful eyes and an unhurried air of there's-absolutely-nothing-to-worry-about!

**Whiskey**
Born premature and bottle fed for several weeks, Rishi's son is a chip off the old block, a little male version of his wonderful mama.

**Benito**
No hurry, no worry, just keep plodding gently on regard-less. A master at somehow burying his way right into the heart of the hay feeder.

**Zach**
Nothing to do but eat and sleep and eat . . . A playful member of the boys club when not otherwise occupied with his dedication to fodder.

## GALLOWAYS

We first brought Galloways to the farm in January of 2015. It was immediately obvious that here was an incredibly docile and well-grounded breed, that spoke of things well-earthed.

They adapted to their new environment remarkably quickly and were approachable right from the very beginning. The most notable impression they made, soon after their arrival, was one of safety. They brought a quality of acceptance and an unhurried acknowledgement of things exactly as they are.

If the Castas are by nature a very reserved breed, the Galloways appear to express a great joy for living. Well-ordered hierarchy is the foundation of herd life for the Galloways. They seem to be, both physically and socially speaking, more rounded and rough around the edges than the Castas. There is very little standing on ceremony with this lot, as is the case with their French farm mates. Theirs is more of a rugby-scrum approach to things as opposed to the almost starchily rigid aloofness that can often be the way for the Casta.

### Origins and history

This ancient breed of cattle were said to be dark, smooth-polled and wavy-haired and for centuries they went unnamed, referred to only as the black cattle of Galloway. From the south-westernmost region of Scotland, a land of winds and damp cold, combined with an undulating terrain of moors, granitic hills, heathery mountain ranges and fertile glens emerged the Galloway breed of cattle.

They became important during the Scoto-Saxon period, and the breeders of Galloways enjoyed the export of cheese and hides. Later the cattle were sold in considerable numbers to English farmers who sent them to Smithfield market after a fattening period on English grass. It is said that the Galloway breed was never crossed with the other breeds.

## Characteristics

The most visible characteristic of the Galloway is their long coat. Serving a dual purpose, the coarse outer coat shields wind and rain, while the soft, fur-like under coat provides insulation and waterproofing. The colour of the coat ranges from the more popular black, to dun (silver through brown), red, white (with dark pigment about the eyes, nose, ears and teats), and the belted (black, dun or red, with a white band around the middle).

'Galloway cattle are generally very docile,' quotes William Youatt, (English researcher, scientist, veterinary surgeon, historian and standard writer on cattle in the early 1800s.) He goes on to say, 'This is a most valuable point about them in every respect. It is rare to find even a bull furious or troublesome.' Galloways are very courageous, however, and if annoyed by dogs or wild animals, they will act in concert, by forming a crescent and jointly attacking.

This is something we've witnessed first-hand when our dogs have at times passed too close to them. On one occasion several years ago, I even saw them attack a number of small lambs who had strayed into their field as they were being moved down the road by a shepherd. I have to say that it was somehow disturbing to see these incredibly calm and habitually docile beings suddenly transformed into forces of destruction. To them, each mother with a calf to protect, the unexpected arrival of the lambs in their midst triggered a truly instinctive reaction. You can take a cow out of nature, but you cannot take nature out of the cow!

## Leith

900 kilograms of pure muscle but not a single gram of aggression or anything that even hints at such goings on. Beautiful big papa.

## Valentine

Undisputed queen and all-round shining diamond, so very soft with her young and us devotees too. A genuine friend for life.

## July

A face that looks as old as the hills, she carries an unruffled sense of aloofness, retaining something for herself and her kind.

## Isi

Restless where food is concerned, first to the hay and a veritable sprinter when pastures new are offered. When her stomach is full, she loves nothing more than a scratch and so many quiet words.

## Paula

One-time rebel and dedicated leg-kicker, has matured into a most caring mother. Has become quite approachable now, discovering a delight in being stroked and spoken to so lovingly.

## Orion
Oh you perfect friend and ally. Source of goodwill and heartfulness, a softly-burning ember of constant warmth.

## Beauty
Rejected at birth but never by those who spend but a minute in her company. Beauty by name and beauty by nature.

## Root
A stocky, bouncing bundle of youthful energy and instigator of endless rough and tumble.

## Lily
So typically Galloway from head to hoof and everything in-between. Expert at the fine art of escapology, ringleader and ignorer of electric fences.

## Balder
Norse hero and sometime young Galloway bull, this boy is, quite simply, a lot of fun to be around.

## Mai
The current baby of the bunch, innocent, alive and as black as black can be. Favours the fifty metre sprint, head down, tail up and body all a-quiver. Love her.

# Acknowledgements

Who to thank, how to thank them and where to begin? Well, let's start with life Itself, without which none of the rest is possible. I'm talking about the ever-eternal, supreme fount and source of all, the inexpressible essence of Isness, the totality of simply being that lies beyond all thought and thinking. Thank you for the very possibility of simply being able to say thank you, which in itself is a miraculous thing!

To Cork of course, the great fool himself, who never failed to be anything but the most gloriously loving idiot. To Mum and Dad, Pete, Nicky, Rhian, Bethany, Ewan, Henry and Jessie and all the Mountjoy clan scattered far and wide.

To my favourite partners in crime, Gabi and Elie (thank God they have inherited something of the idiotic too), to Diana and all the Casas Huguet family, who have shown me nothing but love and warmth from the very first minute.

To the Captain himself (he knows who he is) and the star-dipped Zoe, nothing but unending love. May you both plot a course of peace eternal on the Sea of Smelly Socks.

Franco and Nic, for friendships beyond the known universe.

Thanks without end to the dearest Rev Zachary and all my most beloved Karamojong family, who inspire me daily with their prayers and African spirit.

A huge and everlasting thanks to Jamie, Polly, Abi and the rest of the team at Bedford Square Publishers for taking the plunge and bringing this whole story to the world.

To Paul and Susan at The Feldstein Agency for their perfect support and complete trust in the whole project.

Gill Farrer-Halls, for you I have nothing but the deepest of deep gratitude. Without your brutally honest guidance, the script would have stayed in so many millions of pieces. Your genius at helping me bring structure to the chaos was and is, quite simply, an act of love.

Penny Olivia, without your suggestion that 'You should write a book about all this,' things would be oh so very different. You are a planter of the most wonderful seeds.

And finally, propping up the rest with unwavering steadiness and in perfect tandem with each other, The Maharshi and those fur-covered soulmates otherwise known as the cows. Words fail me.

# About the Author

Dave Mountjoy is a cattle breeder, the founder of Being with Cows Retreats and father of two slightly wild young boys. He is inspired by living in dedication to quietness, to acceptance and the understanding that behind the rough and tumble of everyday life, the unchanging presence of love seeks only to guide us back into the lasting peace of the heart.

Find out more about Dave and the
Being With Cows Retreats online:

**beingwithcows.com**
**@beingwithcows**

**Bedford
Square**
*Publishers*

Bedford Square Publishers is an independent publisher of
fiction and non-fiction, founded in 2022 in the historic
streets of Bedford Square London and the sea mist
shrouded green of Bedford Square Brighton.

Our goal is to discover irresistible stories and voices that
illuminate our world.

We are passionate about connecting our authors to readers
across the globe and our independence allows us to do this
in original and nimble ways.

The team at Bedford Square Publishers has years of
experience and we aim to use that knowledge and creative
insight, alongside evolving technology, to reach the right
readers for our books. From the ones who read a lot, to the
ones who don't consider themselves readers, we aim to find
those who will love our books and talk about them as much
as we do.

We are hunting for vital new voices from all backgrounds –
with books that take the reader to new places and transform
perceptions of the world we live in.

**Follow us on social media for the latest Bedford Square
Publishers news.**

🐦 @bcdsqpublishers
f facebook.com/bedfordsq.publishers/
📷 @bedfordsq.publishers

**https://bedfordsquarepublishers.co.uk/**